YORK NOTES

POETRY OF THE FIRST WORLD WAR

NOTES BY TOM RANK

 Longman

York Press

The right of Tom Rank to be identified as Author of
this Work has been asserted by him in accordance
with the Copyright, Designs and Patents Act 1988

YORK PRESS
322 Old Brompton Road, London SW5 9JH

PEARSON EDUCATION LIMITED
Edinburgh Gate, Harlow,
Essex CM20 2JE, United Kingdom
Associated companies, branches and representatives throughout the world

For permissions and acknowledgements, see p. 158 at the back
of these Notes

First published 2008
Third impression 2009

ISBN 978–1–4058–9618–4

Phototypeset by Chat Noir Design, France
Printed in China

In memory of Lieutenant Sydney Rank, 216th Siege Battery, Royal Garrison Artillery, who died in
France on 23 October 1918

CONTENTS

PART THREE
CRITICAL APPROACHES

PART FOUR
CRITICAL PERSPECTIVES

PART FIVE
BACKGROUND

PART ONE

INTRODUCTION

STUDYING POEMS

Reading poems and exploring them critically can be approached in a number of ways, but when reading a poem for the first time it is a good idea to consider some, or all, of the following:

- **Format and style**: how do poems differ from other genres of text? Does the poem capture a single moment in time, tell a whole story, or make a specific point?

- **The poet's perspective**: consider what the poet has to say, how he or she presents a particular view of people, the world, society, ideas, issues, etc. Are, or were, these views controversial?

- **Verse and metre**: how are **stanzas** or patterns of lines used to reveal the **narrative**? What **rhythms** and **rhymes** does the poet use to convey an atmosphere or achieve an effect?

- **Choice of language**: does the poet choose to write formally or informally? Does he or she use different registers for different voices in the poem, vary the sound and style, employ literary techniques such as **imagery**, **alliteration** and **metaphor**?

- **Links and connections**: what other texts does this poem remind you of? Can you see connections between its narrative, main characters and ideas and those of other texts you have studied? Is the poem part of a literary movement or tradition?

- **Your perspective and that of others**: what are your feelings about the poem? Can you relate to its emotions, themes and ideas? What do others say about the poem – for example, critics or other poets and writers?

These York Notes offer an introduction to the poetry of the First World War and cannot substitute for close reading of the text and the study of secondary sources.

CHECK THE BOOK
A good starting point is Andrew Barlow's *The Great War in British Literature* (Cambridge, 2000). It offers a succinct overview with a brief anthology of poems and extracts from fiction and drama.

READING THE POETRY OF THE FIRST WORLD WAR

CHECK THE POEM

Scannell's 'The Great War' describes how the Great War dominates his perception of war even though he himself fought in the Second World War. You can read the whole of Scannell's poem on pp. 223–4 of *The Oxford Book of War Poetry*.

'War poetry' seems a distinct and obvious classification for twenty-first century readers. Almost everyone will have heard or read, at a ceremony, in a broadcast or poster, or on a war memorial, Lawrence Binyon's lines from 'For the Fallen':

> At the going down of the sun and in the morning
> We will remember them. (15–16)

John McCrae's poem 'In Flanders Fields' became the inspiration for the British Legion's annual poppy campaign and still features in their publicity, whilst Rupert Brooke's 'The Soldier' must be one of the best known poems in English – it was the choice of the Prime Minister, Tony Blair, for inclusion in *The Big Book of Little Poems* in 1999. If these poems are now part of what Andrew Motion in the introduction to his own anthology, *First World War Poems* (2003), calls 'state furniture', along with the two-minute silence on Armistice Day, for most British school and college students a handful of war poets of a rather different kind are just as much part of the classroom furniture – Owen and Sassoon in particular.

Yet war poetry became a recognisable category only as a result of the large number of poems written during and after the First World War, and even today the term still principally suggests writing about what Vernon Scannell calls 'the war that was called Great'. The detailed reasons for this will be explored in later sections of these Notes but the chief causes are obvious: this was not only the first major war for British troops for a hundred years, it was also on such a huge and mechanised scale that very few communities or even families were untouched, as the long lists of the dead on war memorials in many towns and villages still testify. Conscription was introduced in Britain for the first time in 1916, but even before that tens of thousands had enlisted. In the huge army that Kitchener hastily recruited, the professional soldiers were vastly outnumbered by volunteers and conscripts. The officer class had usually received an education founded on the classics and informed by the idealism of Victorian and Edwardian culture. Universal education also meant that private soldiers were, for the first time, literate and acquainted with the English literary tradition, whilst families at home were anxious not only for news but also for anything that would help them make sense of the unfolding conflict.

The war came at a time of great social, political and cultural change which was hastened in turn by the effects of the devastation it brought. The early years of the twentieth century saw the birth of a number of movements in the arts, most notably one that took the title **modernism** and continues to be influential today. This was also a period of industrial and political unrest throughout Europe. In Britain, the most immediate concern for many in 1914 was the possibility of conflict in Ireland, whilst Suffragettes continued to demonstrate in favour of women's rights and strikes indicated strains in the social and economic system. Developments in technology made communication easier and reading matter more accessible to all – but also fed the arms race that led eventually to the industrialised slaughter of the Western Front and to air raids over London. In 1914, Europe plunged into an unprecedented conflict which soon affected all sections of society. Families were actively targeted by recruiting campaigns whilst many women found new kinds of employment at home or behind the lines as nurses or members of the Voluntary Aid Detachment (VAD) – and soon many at home knew the painful realities of bereavement. The impact of the war was felt more widely as fighting spread to the Middle East and troops from the British colonies and former colonies arrived in Europe, joined in 1917 by forces from the USA. This is reflected in Jon Stallworthy's anthology, where 'In Flanders Fields' by the Canadian doctor John McCrae is joined by 'next to you of course god america i / love you land of the pilgrims' by the American E. E. Cummings. No selection can be truly comprehensive and women are rather under-represented in *The Oxford Book of War Poetry*, as is the vast amount of popular verse produced during the war that has largely disappeared since. These Notes will direct you to sources of further reading so that you can extend your knowledge and understanding of the poetry of the First World War.

Poetry was the dominant literary form of the First World War, at least in Britain. Partly no doubt this was because lyric poetry lends

> **CONTEXT**
>
> In a study published in 1978, Catherine Reilly identified 2,225 British writers of the First World War period who published poems about the war in some form. At least 417 served in uniform (such as the armed forces or Red Cross) and at least 532 were women. Of these, only the work of a handful remains in print today.

itself to work in time snatched between combat, work written – like McCrae's famous poem – in haste as a response to immediate experience. Poetry was popular in the press too; Brooke's sonnet 'The Soldier' and Binyon's 'For the Fallen' attained fame after appearing in *The Times*. Other war literature – drama, novels – required more time and the right conditions for writing and production. However, it was also the case that poetry seemed best able to catch the mood not only of the troops but also of the public at large. Edmund Blunden noted wryly that during the war the term 'soldier-poet' was 'almost as familiar as a ration card' and, later, Lord Flasheart in the television series *Blackadder Goes Forth* (1989) complains, 'I'm sick of this damn war – the blood, the noise, the endless poetry.' Poetry was popular in ways that it is hard to appreciate today; newspapers regularly printed new poems and volumes of verse also did well. In 1914 a Georgian Poetry anthology could expect to sell over 20,000 copies in hardback. 'Georgian Poetry' is a term we shall examine in more detail later; it included writers such as Brooke whose verse now seems anchored in the traditions of the pre-war era but it was also a label that a poet like Owen was proud to wear. The Georgians sought to address, at least in part, modern concerns whilst remaining accessible. Other writers, such as Ezra Pound, had already adopted a more consciously hostile stand against the state of poetry and indeed society in the pre-war period. Poetry of both kinds was produced in response to the war. The need for consolation in grief and for a literature that attempted to make sense of the deaths of so many meant that there was an audience for both formal and informal poetry of a kind that offered traditional forms as well as traditional certainties. Others felt that the unprecedented horrors that the war was unleashing on Western civilisation required a new, more urgent, response. When life itself seemed senseless, art must reflect this. Wilfred Owen, in words he drafted for an introduction to his poetry though never completed, went so far as to write: 'Above all I am not concerned with Poetry. My subject is War, and the pity of War.' A selection of war poetry is likely to include celebration, mourning and protest – but it should also be concerned with poetry.

One value of an anthology like *The Oxford Book of War Poetry* is that it reveals the wide variety of responses to the First World War.

 QUESTION

What factors do you think influence editors and publishers when making decisions about which poems to include in an anthology or collection?

Readers acquainted with the work of a few popular 'trench poets' will hear not only familiar voices from the front but also other accents, always interesting and sometimes surprising, whether it is the Irish accent Yeats gives to his responses or the sardonic tone of the American poet E. E. Cummings. Stallworthy's complete anthology also provides an opportunity to see some of the kinds of poetry which would have been familiar to readers and poets in 1914 and to consider the effect of the First World War on later poets. You can read more about this in **Part Five: Literary background.**

QUESTION

What does the term 'war poetry' mean to you? Which poems and poets come to mind? Can you say where these ideas come from? As you read the poems covered in these Notes, consider how far your preconceptions are challenged and what further reading you might need to do for a more balanced understanding of poetry of the First World War.

PART TWO

THE TEXT

NOTE ON THE TEXT

The poems explored in these Notes are all found in *The Oxford Book of War Poetry*, edited by Jon Stallworthy and first published by Oxford University Press in 1984. Page numbers refer to the 2003 paperback edition, where the First World War section occupies pages 160–225. Where relevant, information is provided about when and where the poems were first published. Further information can be found in the brief notes Stallworthy provides at the back of the anthology. Many of these poems appear in other collections of First World War poetry such as Brian Gardner's *Up the Line to Death*, first published by Methuen in 1964; *Men Who March Away*, edited by I. M. Parsons and first published by Heinemann in 1965; Jon Silkin's *Penguin Book of First World War Poetry* (1979) and *Never Such Innocence*, published in 1988 and now available in an Everyman edition. Stallworthy includes poems by two women whose work, along with poems by many other women, can be found in Catherine Reilly's *Scars Upon My Heart* (Virago, 1981). Further details of these, other collections and suggestions for further reading can be found in **Part Five: Background** and **Further reading**.

DETAILED SUMMARIES

THOMAS HARDY: MEN WHO MARCH AWAY

- Volunteers marching to war tell those who watch them pass by of their faith in the justice of their cause.

The first two **stanzas** of the poem are in the form of questions by the 'men who march away' (2) to war in the early morning light. Those with 'musing eye' (9) who watch them pass may wonder

CHECK THE POEM

Hardy had written a number of poems about war before 1914. 'Drummer Hodge' and 'The Man He Killed', both about the Boer (South African) War, deal with death in battle in a way that the two First World War poems here do not. You can find them on pp. 150f. of *The Oxford Book of War Poetry*.

what has motivated these soldiers. Have they been tricked into joining the army by a 'purblind prank' (8)? The remaining three stanzas contain their answer. They go to war because their country needs them; they believe victory will be theirs because the cause is just.

COMMENTARY

In this poem, first published in *The Times* on 5 September 1914 (just a month after the outbreak of war), Hardy appears to abandon his usual **ironic** view of events to write what is almost a recruiting song. The jaunty **rhythm**, aided by **alliteration** and reinforced by repetition of phrases such as 'faith and fire' (1), gives the poem a marching feel well suited to its subject. The simple style suits Hardy's straightforward message, that 'Victory crowns the just' (23). The final stanza, almost word for word identical to the first, affirms the soldiers' confidence. More typical of Hardy are the rural references, such as the reference to 'barn-cocks' (3 and 31), and the phrase 'purblind prank' (8), which is a reminder that in his long verse drama *The Dynasts* of 1904–8 he refers to an impersonal controlling mind, an 'It' that is unconscious of the sufferings of the humans in its power. Here, however, Hardy rejects the idea that the soldiers are going blindly to their fate – 'We well see what we are doing' they repeat (15 and 20) – and he does not contradict them.

GLOSSARY		
8	**purblind**	nearly blind, dim-witted
24	**braggarts**	boasters

THOMAS HARDY: IN TIME OF 'THE BREAKING OF NATIONS'

- The routines of life and love continue during the conflict, and will continue long after it is over.

The poem describes three archetypal rural scenes: a man and his horse working in a field, a smouldering mound of grass and a pair of

CONTEXT

The poet Charles Sorley (1895–1915) attacked Hardy's view that the just will be rewarded: 'I think that "Men who March Away" is the most arid poem in the book besides being untrue of the sentiments of the ranksman going to war: "Victory crowns the just" is the worst line he ever wrote – filched from a leading article in *The Morning Post* and unworthy of him who had always previously disdained to insult Justice by offering it a material crown like Victor' (letter of 30 November 1914). Two of Sorley's poems appear on pp. 166–7 in *The Oxford Book of War Poetry*.

QUESTION

Jon Silkin writes: 'One would have expected Hardy to have been among the first to see that despite love's eternal recurrence, war in many cases terminates the relationships which make up the total "eternal" story. Seen in this light, the conclusion of Hardy's poem has a slightly facile ring' (*Out of Battle*, Routledge, 1987, p. 54). Do you agree with this view?

CHECK THE POEM

Hardy had written about a husband's death in war in 'A Wife in London' in 1899 (*The Oxford Book of War Poetry*, p. 150). For another poem which contrasts rural life and love with the war, see Edward Thomas's 'As the team's head brass' (p. 180).

lovers. These represent the continuing cycle of life that will long outlive war.

COMMENTARY

The title of the poem is a reference to the words of the Old Testament prophet Jeremiah: 'with thee I will break in pieces the nations' (Jeremiah 51:12). The war is referred to directly only in the penultimate line of this short poem, an indication of the poet's view of its relative importance. Hardy, whose novels and poems are firmly grounded in rural life, evokes the three scenes economically; his repetition of 'only' in the first line of **stanzas** I and II, seems to imply these are unremarkable scenes hardly worthy of comment. His description of the 'silent walk' (2) of the 'half asleep' (4) horse and the 'thin smoke' (5) of grass that is merely smouldering could indicate a dying way of life, but his use of 'Yet' in line 7 marks the contradiction: this humble, unremarkable existence will continue whilst 'Dynasties pass' (8). The final stanza is a kind of recapitulation, with the young lovers (referred to in archaic terms as 'a maid and her wight' (9) to stress the timeless nature of the scene) contrasted to 'war's annals', which will pass. Its affirmation of the longevity of love is in contrast to the ominous title, which implies only destruction. The short lines and simple **rhyme** scheme are well matched to the simplicity of the scenes Hardy describes.

GLOSSARY		
9	**wight**	an archaic term for a man
11	**annals**	historical records

RUPERT BROOKE: PEACE

- The sonnet is an expression of thanks for being able to respond to the call to arms and leave behind the stale and empty concerns of civilian life.
- It ends with willingness to accept death.

The poet greets the advent of war as a call to wake from the sleep of dull civilian life. The world is 'weary' (5); he urges his listeners to leave those who will not heed the appeal to 'honour' (6), for they are less than real men, he implies, and even love is empty. The **sestet** addresses the consequences of war, which is seen as 'release' from 'shame' (9). The suffering is described as temporary and death is described as a friend as well as an enemy.

COMMENTARY

This is the first of three of Brooke's **sonnets** printed in *The Oxford Book of War Poetry*. Brooke's enthusiasm is clear from the first line, where the conversational 'Now' is followed by an expression of gratitude to God for the privilege of responding to the call to arms and the new simplicity that the call offers. In place of 'dirty songs' (7), there is 'cleanness' (4); 'half-men' (7) are spurned for the youth and power of 'clear eye, and sharpened power' (3). The **rhetoric** is powerful and the sonnet's construction is effective, ending as it does with the neat **paradox** that Death is the 'worst friend' as well as an 'enemy' (14).

The sonnet opens on a religious note, with capital letters for the pronouns referring to God. Later, it is only 'Death' who is dignified in this way (14). (Brooke's wording may be an unconscious and **ironic** echo of Martin Rinkart's German hymn, well known in English as 'Now thank we all our God'.) Brooke's description of 'swimmers into cleanness leaping' (4), with the verb placed at the end of the line for most effect, emphasises his view of the world that will be left behind by those brave enough. His dismissal of those unmoved by the call to honour is part of **martial rhetoric**, the exalted language of the warrior, but there is also a note of contempt for other aspects of life that is less usual. Whatever kind of love the poet sees as being 'little emptiness' (8), this is not the usual language of the warrior as lover and defender of loved ones. Line 9 goes so far as to refer to 'shame'; it seems that the war is a chance to leave behind the confusions and failures of the poet's own life, which could be seen to conflict with the reference to 'honour' earlier (6). The sestet uses a series of negatives ('no ill, no grief … naught broken … nothing', 10–12) as an indication of the attitude to suffering and death – the suffering, even 'agony' (13) is, the language

CHECK THE POEM

Brooke was not the only poet to express distaste for the pre-war world. The American poet Ezra Pound, in *Hugh Selwyn Mauberley* (p. 210), writes of 'a botched civilization', though his bitterness is coloured by knowledge that 'There died a myriad, And of the best' (14, 11–12).

QUESTION

Why do you think Brooke called his sonnet 'Peace'? Where, do you think, does he feel he will be at peace?

makes clear, only temporary. The poet welcomes death as the 'heart's long peace' (12); it is Death which is the last word of the sonnet.

RUPERT BROOKE: THE DEAD

www. CHECK THE NET
The text of all Brooke's '1914' sonnets can be found on Oxford University's First World War Poetry Digital Archive, along with notes and useful links, at **www.ww1lit.com.** Find these resources in the 'Education Area'.

- The poem celebrates those who have given their lives – the sacrifice of the most lowly of them has given the world honour and nobility.

Brooke's poem comments on those who have given up everything that the future might have held for them. They have bought with their sacrifices precious gifts that they offer us – holiness, love, pain, honour and nobility are again seen in our land.

COMMENTARY

This is the third of Brooke's war **sonnets** and begins with a military reference to 'bugles' (line 1). The term, recalling a military funeral, has an archaic ring and is probably a deliberate echo of Tennyson's repeated invocation, 'blow, bugle, blow', from 'The splendour falls on castle walls', particularly when Brooke repeats the command at the beginning of the **sestet**. Like Tennyson (1809–92), Brooke makes many references to chivalry. Apart from the 'Dead' themselves (1), the gifts they bring are honoured with capital letters: 'Holiness … and Love, and Pain. / Honour … and Nobleness' (10–13). The value of heroic sacrifice is stressed by the vocabulary, which speaks of the 'rich Dead' (1), however 'lonely and poor', in their previous life (2) who die in conflict to give 'rarer gifts than gold' (3). Brooke says that they consciously 'laid the world away' (4) – the world that, in 'Peace', Brooke had called 'old and cold and weary' – and offered themselves as sacrifices. The words 'poured out the red / Sweet wine of youth' (4–5) continue this emphasis by recalling an offering to the gods of classical antiquity rather than death in modern battle. There is no feeling, as with later poets, that these deaths were needless waste, though Brooke does acknowledge the extent of their losses: they will have no long, happy life and peaceful old age and no 'sons' (8). (This sonnet, like 'Peace', has a masculine emphasis: only in 'The Soldier' does Brooke use a feminine reference, when England is viewed as a kind of mother.)

The **chivalric** references continue in the sestet, where the heroic virtues are seen in regal terms ('Honour has come back, as a king, to earth', 11). Along with these **personified** qualities ('Nobleness walks in our ways again', 13), Brooke includes both 'Love, and Pain' (10), emphasising perhaps the suffering that is necessary to attain this new state of purity. The conjunction is, however, a little awkward, since whilst it is easy to visualise kingly Honour, Pain hardly seems a virtue or quality but rather something that one suffers, nor is it normally something we would feel a 'dearth' of, as line 9 implies. Brooke's final line talks of 'our heritage', which presumably means the new state of nobility and heroism won for us by the dead. Who 'we' are is not specified, but in the context of the sonnet sequence we can assume Brooke means the English nation, with perhaps a sense of returning to the time of King Arthur. This final word completes the references to payment and rewards which began with the word 'rich' in the first line, though the heritage seems to be our reward for the payment made by those who die and is therefore not strictly our own, as 'wage' in line 12 would imply. Like Brooke's other sonnets, the **rhetorical** devices and easy fluency convey an unquestioning confidence in the value of sacrifice that does not always sustain close analysis of his words. This is particularly the case for modern readers familiar, as Brooke could not be, with the later horrors of the war and with the work of poets such as Owen and Sassoon who addressed the suffering in quite different ways.

GLOSSARY

9	dearth scarceness, shortage of something

CONTEXT

Brooke's sonnet sequence entitled '1914' was published in 1915 after Brooke had seen brief action as an officer in the Navy. After his death on the way to Gallipoli on 23 April 1915 (St George's Day), Winston Churchill wrote in a tribute in *The Times*: 'The thoughts to which he gave expression in the very few incomparable war sonnets which he has left behind will be shared by many thousands of young men moving resolutely and blithely forward into this, the hardest, cruellest, and the least-rewarded of all the wars that men have fought.'

RUPERT BROOKE: THE SOLDIER

CHECK THE POEM
Rupert Brooke's 'The Soldier' from January 1915 is probably the most famous poem indicating a willingness to die for England. In a similar vein, John Freeman declares 'Happy is England in the brave that die' in 'Happy is England Now' (*Up the Line to Death*, p. 8). Jessie Pope asks 'Who'll swell the victor's ranks?' (*Scars Upon My Heart*, p. 88). For a contrast, see how Owen in 'Futility' (p. 193) refers to 'the kind old sun' before crying out in protest that 'fatuous sunbeams' created life at all.

- A soldier reflects that, should he die, his grave will become a little piece of England in a foreign country.

A soldier-poet, addressing those he leaves behind, says that if he dies his grave will be claimed for England. His body, even in the grave, will somewhere give back all those English qualities that he has absorbed during his life. These include both the beauties of the countryside ('flowers ... rivers ... suns of home', 6–8) and what he sees as English values ('laughter ... and gentleness', 13).

COMMENTARY

The final poem in Brooke's sequence is the most famous, regularly recited from the time when the Dean of St Paul's Cathedral first brought it to public attention from his pulpit on Easter Sunday in 1915. It is suitably **oratorical**; the idea of the soldier's grave being claimed as English soil is easy to grasp and illustrated by a series of images of idyllic English countryside and qualities. In Hardy's 'Drummer Hodge' (p. 149), which also reflects on an English soldier's death overseas, a 'portion of that unknown plain / Will Hodge for ever be' (13–14) but in Brooke's poem the grave will be not just the soldier but 'England', a kind of extension of the Empire. (As often in First World War poems, 'England' is referred to rather than 'Britain'; there is more about this in **Themes: Patriotism**.) There is, however, some tension between the patriotic and the personal, as the critic D. J. Enright noted: 'The reiteration of England and "English" is all very well; but an odd uncertainty as to whether the poet is praising England or himself – "a richer dust" [line 4] – remains despite that reiteration' (*The Penguin Guide to English Literature, The Modern Age*). In his **sonnets**, Brooke frequently uses the device of linking aspects in groups of three for **rhetorical** emphasis. In line 5, 'England bore, shaped, and made aware' his body; similarly, he concludes with further triplets in the last three lines, ending on a suitably idealistic and patriotic note with the words 'an English heaven'

Brooke's view of death makes no overt reference to the afterlife other than the claim that the 'dust' (4) of the 'foreign field' (2) will become part of England and the idea, in line 10, that the soldier will be 'a pulse in the eternal mind'. This lack of reference to anything other than an implied belief in life after death (as opposed to any specific religious creed) is another aspect of the sonnet's expression of public, patriotic devotion rather than personal belief. It is also symptomatic of the general nature of Brooke's references to England; the 'sights and sounds' (12), the 'flowers' of line 6 and the other aspects he mentions are, like the 'dreams' of line 12, abstract, unspecified. There is no sense that Brooke is attached to any particular part of the English countryside – in contrast, say, to Ivor Gurney's reference to the 'infinite lovely chatter of Bucks accent' in 'The Silent One' (p. 182) or Edward Thomas's 'fallen elm' in the field in 'As the team's head brass' (p. 180), or even to the details in Julian Grenfell's 'Into Battle' (p. 164).

QUESTION

The poet Charles Sorley said of Brooke's poems in a letter in April 1915: 'He has clothed his attitudes in fine words: but he has taken the sentimental attitude.' How do you respond to Brooke's sonnets, and what factors influence your views?

HERBERT ASQUITH: THE VOLUNTEER

- The poem celebrates a city clerk whose dreams of military glory have been fulfilled.
- His death in battle is rewarded with a place alongside the heroes of the Battle of Agincourt.

The poem takes the form of a tribute to a dead soldier. Although his civilian life had been spent in a dull office, Asquith says he dreamt of the excitement of deeds of heroism in times long passed. Now he has achieved his wish by dying in battle, happy to be able to join the ranks of those who fought for the glory of their country.

COMMENTARY

The title of Asquith's poem reminds the reader that this man had willingly left his dull life 'in a city grey' (2) in search of the excitement that until now had only been a dream based on old legends. The language emphasises this contrast: his life as a clerk is described as 'toiling' and 'grey' (2), 'his days would drift away' (3);

whereas his 'bright eyes' (5) see images of 'legions', 'horsemen' and 'the oriflamme' (6–8). All these evoke ancient values of **chivalry** and **romance** (exciting adventures of ancient heroes) and this tone is continued in the second **stanza**, where the dead soldier goes 'to the halls of dawn' (10) in 'that high hour' (12), so that he is worthy to join 'the men of Agincourt' (16). This **imagery** distances the death in battle from the realities of modern warfare and places it in a mythical past, in which the Roman legions and medieval knights both feature; even his death is described with the words 'his lance is broken' (11).

The structure is straightforward; the two eight-line stanzas mirror each other, linked by the 'And' of line 9. The **rhyme** scheme, with its end-stopped lines linked in a regular pattern, creates a neat sense of finality to the final word, 'Agincourt', transforming the humble clerk and volunteer into a hero like those soldiers Shakespeare's Henry V describes, in words familiar to almost every schoolchild at the time, as 'we happy few, we band of brothers'. As a result, the dead man is awarded a place in the roll of honour of those who have preserved the honour and glory of England. The poem therefore takes its place alongside others from the early period of the war which emphasise the nobility of sacrifice in defence of the country. Paul Fussell, in *The Great War and Modern Memory* (p. 59), notes that, consciously or not, Asquith has placed the soldier's death at 'twilight' (10), when he goes to 'the halls of dawn'; sunrise and sunset were the times of 'stand-to', when the armies on both sides of the line stood facing the opposite trenches watching for any sign of an attack.

CHECK THE POEM

You might like to compare 'The Volunteer', written in May 1915, with another poem by Herbert Asquith from later in the war, 'After the Salvo', which appears in *Up the Line to Death* (p. 81). There, in contrast to the certainty of glory, he asks: 'Have we lost our way / Or are we toys of a god at play / We who do these things on a young spring day?'

GLOSSARY		
8	**oriflamme** a banner of red silk split into points and carried on a gilt staff or lance, adopted as the national banner of France in the Middle Ages	
16	**Agincourt** British victory over the French army in 1415, celebrated in Shakespeare's *Henry V*	

JULIAN GRENFELL: INTO BATTLE

- The poem celebrates spring and moves on to describe the vitality of the warrior, whose sacrifice will be rewarded.
- Nature and the soldier are at one and this gives him peace and a sense of destiny.

The poem opens with a celebration of spring and its sense of new life. The second stanza links this to the warrior's dedication to his cause as he draws strength from nature and finds in death new life when he joins 'the bright company of Heaven' (15). The trees and birds in their own ways bid the warrior be strong, bold and keen, and he draws comfort from the patience of the horses waiting for battle to begin. The poem concludes with a sense of destiny: death will come only to those who are chosen; live or die, he will be safe.

COMMENTARY

This poem shares its idealistic attitude towards war with a number of others from the early period of the war, including those by Brooke and Asquith in the *The Oxford Book of War Poetry*. Alongside the dedication to sacrifice and the sense of the excitement of battle, however, it also has a sense of the vividness of the natural world even though Grenfell sees nature as urging him to be strong and sure in battle rather than lamenting, as later poets would, the destruction of life. The realities of conflict are hinted at only with the words 'lead' and 'steel' (41); the other references, to physical valour and to cavalry horses, link the poem to heroic attitudes to war from an earlier age that in the light of later poetry sound remote and archaic.

The opening stanza conveys the energy of spring by the use of words such as 'bursting' and 'quivers'. The second stanza moves to a more general reference to 'life' and 'light' and from this to the soldier's own energy which is likened to nature's 'striving' (6). This is given urgency by the **anaphoric** pattern to the stanza ('And … And …'). The extension of the third stanza to six lines brings this

CHECK THE POEM
Hardy's 'Channel Firing', about naval gunnery practice in April 1914, shows his prescience about 'all nations striving strong to make / Red war yet redder'. It forms the Prelude in the anthology *Up the Line to Death* and is also the first poem in Andrew Motion's collection *First World War Poems* (Faber, 2003).

CHECK THE BOOK

Bernard Bergonzi writes: '"Into Battle" is the last memorable verbal enactment of that [**romantic** and **chivalric**] attitude in English literature: the poetic equivalent of some final, anachronistic battle in which cavalry (etymologically close to chivalry) played a dominant part' (*Heroes' Twilight*, 1996, p. 45).

section of the poem to a conclusion, in which the warrior takes energy and life force from nature and then finds 'great rest' (14) after battle. The last word of the third **stanza**, 'dearth', despite its closeness to 'death', conveys the belief that 'fullness' comes to those who perish, a satisfaction of hunger. Grenfell does not specify exactly what the soldier longs for, though line 8 asserts, in apparent contradiction to logic, that 'who dies fighting has increase', implying that the warrior's inheritance is fame or glory. This is developed in the fourth stanza, where the soldier, like a hero in classical mythology, joins the 'bright company of Heaven' in 'high comradeship' (15–16). The fifth stanza reverts to a description of nature as in the opening and it is only in the conclusion of the next stanza that the reader realises that Grenfell is using nature as encouragement to the warrior, as the blackbird does in the seventh stanza, where the short final line emphasises the urgency of the exhortation. The battle is hinted at in terms such as 'brazen frenzy' (32) and 'burning moment' (35), both of which imply trial or refining in a furnace, just as the bird's song earlier implies the conflict is a kind of performance – made explicit by the words 'joy of battle' in line 37. The final stanza continues the idea of a protecting providence that Grenfell asserts in line 42. The word 'thundering' (43) conveys the power of battle and the verbs in the next line reinforce this; against these threats Grenfell places 'clasp' in the middle of the penultimate line and 'fold' in an echo of that sentence in the last line to emphasise that the warrior will be protected, whether by being plucked from danger or wrapped in the 'soft wings' of 'Night', Grenfell's **euphemism** for death.

GLOSSARY

17–18	**Dog-Star, Sisters Seven and Orion's Belt** names of constellations in the night sky

JOHN MCCRAE: IN FLANDERS FIELDS

- The dead, lying beneath ground covered with poppies, urge the living to continue the struggle against the enemy.

McCrae gives voice to the dead in a war cemetery. Above them poppies flourish and the larks fly, though the sound of gunfire drowns their songs. The dead, who so recently enjoyed the beauties of nature, appeal to the living to take up the fight against the enemy or they will not be able to rest at peace beneath the poppies.

COMMENTARY

McCrae assumes the voice of 'the Dead' (6) lying in one of the many cemeteries near the front line. At first, it seems that they are at peace, the poppies **symbolising** both shed blood because of their red colour and sleep though their associations with opium (as a doctor, McCrae would have used the opiate morphine to ease the sufferings of the wounded). The **pastoral** imagery, with its sense of peace and the beauty of nature, is maintained by the references to 'larks' in line 4 and 'dawn' and 'sunset' in the second stanza, though McCrae has also reminded us in line 5 that the sound of the guns drowns out the birdsong. The **elegiac** tone is reinforced by the choice of language; the larks are given heroic attributes, 'still bravely singing', as though driven by a force that even the guns cannot defeat, the sunset 'glows' and the dead once 'loved and were loved' (8), just like the living. The references to dawn and sunset would have an extra resonance for those with experience of the front, for these were the times of 'stand-to', when every soldier would peer anxiously over No Man's Land for any signs of activity or attack by the enemy opposite (see also **Herbert Asquith: The Volunteer**).

The tone changes markedly in the final stanza. From merely describing their feelings and their fate, the dead turn to the living, challenging them to 'take up our quarrel with the foe' (10). The pastoral imagery gives way to 'the torch' (11), an ostensibly awkward image in the setting of trench warfare, since it is clear McCrae means an old-fashioned flaming torch. It is a reminder

CONTEXT

McCrae wrote 'In Flanders Fields' outside his dressing station near Ypres on 3 May 1915. A young friend and former student had been killed the day before and McCrae performed the brief burial ceremony in complete darkness that night. The poem was very nearly lost. Dissatisfied with it, McCrae threw it away, but his commanding officer rescued the draft and sent it to England. It was published in *Punch* magazine on 8 December 1915 and became one of the most popular poems of the war.

? QUESTION

In the last six lines, says Paul Fussell, 'we suddenly have a recruiting-poster rhetoric apparently applicable to any war' (*The Great War and Modern Memory*, p. 249). How do you react to the appeal of McCrae's final lines? Do you think he has made a case for continuing the 'quarrel'?

perhaps of medieval **chivalry** (courage, honour and the like) or Henry Newbolt's 'Vitaï Lampada' (*The Oxford Book of War Poetry*, p. 146), where the schoolboy cries as he 'bear[s] though life like a torch in flame ... "Play up! Play up! and play the game!"' The listener is no longer assumed to be merely sympathetic; McCrae seems to demand acceptance of the challenge. Unless we respond, he claims, the dead will not sleep, for all the sleepy beauty of the poppies above them.

Stylistically the poem is interesting. McCrae's commanding officer, Lieutenant-Colonel Edward Morrison, wrote: 'I have a letter from him in which he mentions having written the poem to pass away the time between the arrival of batches of wounded, and partly as an experiment with several varieties of poetic metre.' The smooth **metre** of the first five lines, aided by the tight **rhyme** scheme (there are only two rhymes in the whole poem, with just the **refrain** unrhymed) and the **enjambement** at the end of three of the lines, conveys the sense that the dead are at peace. This is disturbed by the short syllables and abrupt **caesura** in the first line of the second **stanza**: 'We are the Dead'. McCrae reminds us that theirs is no ordinary sleep, emphasising this by the use of the capital 'D' to give added importance to the fallen. However, although the metre is now more broken, the second stanza concludes with a short line that seems to stress the finality of death, with the placing of the word 'lie' at the end of the penultimate line reinforcing this. The final stanza is more stirring, the language has elements of the archaic, perhaps to aid its appeal to ancient heroism, as the hearer is addressed as 'ye' (13, though it has been 'you', line 11). Again McCrae uses the short line as a refrain to emphasise his appeal.

Using the voices of the dead was not new. In particular, Thomas Hardy's 'Channel Firing', written just before the war in April 1914, deploys voices of those in a graveyard shaken by gunnery practice at sea to comment **ironically** on the enduring folly of war (Brian Gardner uses it as the prefatory poem for his anthology *Up the Line to Death*). Even more significant is the poppy **motif**, to which McCrae's poem contributed. Already a symbol of both life and death because of its blood-red petals and black heart, the poppy features in a number of other First World War poems, most notably perhaps in Isaac Rosenberg's 'Break of Day in the Trenches' (p. 184). McCrae's poem also makes interesting comparison with the two poems by Charles Sorley which follow it in the anthology, and with Ivor Gurney's use of flowers in 'To His Love' (p. 181).

 CHECK THE NET
Rob Ruggenberg's *Heritage of the Great War* site has an interesting account of how McCrae came to write this poem, together with a copy of the manuscript, a sketch of the cemetery and other information about McCrae. Go to **www.greatwar.nl**

> ### GLOSSARY
>
> Title   Flanders   the area in Belgium and northern France where British and Canadian troops held the line against the Germans

CHARLES SORLEY: 'ALL THE HILLS AND VALES ALONG'

- Addressing men marching past, the poet urges them to sing while they have life.
- The earth will welcome them in death just as it has welcomed everyone else who has passed by.

This poem, sometimes given the title 'Route March', describes a column of men who sing as they march by. The poet urges them to enjoy the moment, for the earth will take them when they are dead just as it has famous figures from the past.

COMMENTARY

The poem's jaunty **rhythm**, powerfully suggesting the marching song of the soldiers, is in stark contrast with the tone Sorley adopts in his regular reminders to the men that soon many of them will be dead. This is clear in the first four lines, in which the neat rhyme of 'along' and 'song' in the first two lines is matched by the pairing of the jocular word 'chaps' (3) with the ironic phrase 'who are going to die perhaps' (4). The word order here emphasises the casual nature of fate ('perhaps') rather than any destined glory. This is taken up in the second stanza with the exhortation to 'Cast away regret and rue' (9), with the **alliteration** seeming to make light of these feelings – since, Sorley implies, there is no point in being regretful when it is death 'you are marching to' (10). He mentions some famous figures from the past who have died: the earth absorbed both Jesus Christ and Socrates because, as the four-times repeated pattern in the third stanza makes clear, the earth is happy to make use of the dead bodies. This reaches a climax in the last line of this **stanza**, with the brutal link: 'So be merry, so be dead.' The sharp **caesura**, dividing the line in half, makes the fate of the men – cheerfulness or death – seem arbitrary. This is the point made earlier, when Sorley mentions that Jesus 'died' but Barabbas (the criminal) 'went his way' (14). The line is repeated in the final line of the poem, as if to ensure that the men do not miss the message.

The vigorous **rhythm** is conveyed through a regular pattern of verse and **chorus**, though the 'verses', unlike those in a traditional marching song, are of uneven length and the final 'chorus' has six lines rather than the four of the previous three. This allows Sorley to vary his emphasis. In the third stanza he dwells on the indifference of the earth about who dies. The final stanza returns to the vigorous beat of the opening, with the tumbling list of 'Ringing swinging glad song-throwing' (8) making their music sound full of rowdy life – yet this is countered by the switch to the sombre, run-on line: 'when foot / Lies numb and voice mute' (37–8). The final six lines recall the pattern of previous choruses, with 'gladness' occurring in all of them. First they were to 'give' their gladness (7), then 'pour' it (like sacrificial blood, 18 and 29) and finally 'strew' it (43), carelessly, as if their lives had little value. The attitude to death is in contrast to Grenfell's and McCrae's in the poems which precede it in the *The Oxford Book of War Poetry*, though Sorley, whilst not glorifying death, sees nature as indifferent and the role of men in killing is not addressed.

CHECK THE POEM

Sorley spent some time in Germany in 1914, planning to study at the University of Jena, and admired German culture. In his poem 'To Germany', which can be found in *Up the Line to Death*, p. 46, he writes 'You are blind like us' and speaks of a reconciliation 'when it is peace'.

GLOSSARY

12	**Barabbas** rebel and criminal who was released by Pontius Pilate in preference to Jesus Christ
22	**Hemlock** poisonous plant; made into a drink, it was given to the ancient Greek philosopher Socrates for corrupting the minds of the youth of Athens

CHARLES SORLEY: 'WHEN YOU SEE MILLIONS OF THE MOUTHLESS DEAD'

- The poet tells the reader not to be deceived about the dead.
- Their existence is so far removed from ours that it does not matter what we think or say of them.

The poet advises the reader who dreams of the dead not to be concerned about remembering them. Nothing the living say or feel, whether praise or grief, will make any difference. Even if you seem to recognise a face in the dream, it will not be the person you knew: Sorley suggests that the dead are all completely cut off from the living.

COMMENTARY

This **sonnet** has an apparently simple idea at its heart: that the dead are dead, and any dreams we may have of honouring or remembering them make no difference whatsoever. Sorley's final two lines take this to its conclusion: it is not possible to communicate with or even recognise anyone after death. What gives the poem its power is the simplicity with which Sorley patiently explains this. It is as though he is mindful of the various kinds of self-deception that the living practise and is correcting them one by one. It makes no difference whether or not you 'remember' (4), nor whether you praise them or not – for they cannot hear you (5). They have no concern for our 'tears' (7) or 'honour' (8). His argument culminates in the bald statement 'It is easy to be dead' at the end of the **octave**. The **sestet** repeats and simplifies this even further, 'They are dead' (9), and, to make it clear that death is far from exceptional, adds that 'many a better one has died before' (10).

Sorley's style is far more sombre here than in 'All the hills and vales along'. The uncommon word 'mouthless' in the opening line is arresting, particularly when linked by **alliteration** to 'millions' to remind the reader how common death is. Sorley may have been anticipating the extent of the slaughter that was only beginning when he died in 1915 or may instead have been seeing those who

CHECK THE BOOK

Sorley's poem, stating that the dead are far beyond the reach of the living, is in contrast to the revival of interest in spiritualism during and after the First World War. See Jay Winter's *Sites of Memory, Sites of Mourning* (Cambridge, 1995), a book which examines the ways Europe sought to come to terms with the huge death toll of the war.

QUESTION

Jon Silkin (*Out of Battle*, p. 82) sees the words 'Say only this, "They are dead"' as a comment on Brooke's 'If I should die, think only this of me' in 'The Soldier'. How does Sorley's attitude contrast with Brooke's?

had recently died in war as part of the dead down the ages. The word 'battalions' (2) certainly gives the poem a military reference and the image of 'each gashed head' (6) reminds us of battle wounds. The dream-like feel of the vision he evokes by specific reference in line 2 is maintained by adjectives such as 'pale' (2), 'soft' (3) and 'spook' (13). He uses repetition and contrast: the dead are indifferent alike to 'praise' and 'curses'; 'blind', they do not 'see'; 'deaf' they do not hear us (5–7). The **octave** of the **sonnet** ends in two lines beginning 'Nor' to emphasise that both grief and glory are of no interest to the dead, whatever others might say. Structurally, many of the lines are broken by **caesurae** into two, as if to stress the many ways in which the dead are cut off from the living; lines 7 and 8, for example, divide very unequally after the first two words. However, the first three lines are more even and the sense runs across the first two lines as if to suggest a slow panorama of the dead seen in a dream. The final line returns to this more even **rhythm** to bring a sense of closure to Sorley's argument, ending the sonnet with the finality of 'evermore'.

A. E. HOUSMAN: EPITAPH ON AN ARMY OF MERCENARIES

- The poem describes those who defended their country in return for pay.

Housman's **epitaph** pays tribute to the mercenaries who, in time of need, died in the defence of their country.

COMMENTARY

Housman takes the accusation that the British soldiers were merely interested in pay and makes it into a badge of virtue. The last word of the first **stanza** reminds the reader that they not only received their wages but are also now 'dead'. The last word of the poem is 'pay' but, with a play on 'sum of money', he declares that they 'saved the sum of things'. He has already made clear how desperate was their country's need: 'heaven was falling' (1) and 'earth's foundations fled' (2); in line 7 he goes so far as to imply that 'God abandoned' the nation. The poet's attitude is perhaps clearest in line 5, where the mercenaries, like Atlas in Greek mythology, 'held the sky suspended'. Housman's apparently dismissive references to money are countered by the assertion that these men achieved the impossible. He does this in lines of deceptive simplicity, with a straightforward **rhyme** scheme that links, for example, the dire situation ('foundations fled', 2) to their sacrifice ('dead', 4). The last two lines make telling use of the caesura, contrasting 'abandoned' with 'defended' and introducing the suggestion of a pause before his final, **ironic** use of 'for pay', as though mere money were reward enough for upholding, as he implies, the very foundations of the nation.

CARL SANDBURG: GRASS

- The grass tells how it will soon cover the bodies of the dead, just as it has those who fell in all previous wars.

The grass that grows on a number of battlefields speaks to the reader. It asks for the bodies from a series of battles from Napoleonic times to the First World War to be buried and it will soon hide them. In a few years the battlefields will be overgrown and unrecognisable to passers-by.

COMMENTARY

This short **free-verse** poem expresses the indifference of nature to the loss of life in battle. In casual tone, Sandburg has the grass say: 'Pile the bodies ... pile them high' (1, 4, 5), then 'shovel them under' (6) as if they were just refuse, manure – which, of course, they will soon become. His list of famous battles from European and American history emphasises that history soon moves on. This is illustrated in line 7: 'Two years, ten years' – it doesn't really matter, very soon the grass will have covered the place where so many died. The isolation of the short last two lines from the rest of the poem, repeating in slightly different words the third line, ends the poem on a sombre, almost desolate, note.

CHECK THE POEM
Housman was apparently responding to German propaganda that claimed British soldiers were hired mercenaries. Hugh McDiarmid, in 'Another Epitaph on an Army of Mercenaries' (p. 168), retorted bitterly: 'It is a God-damned lie ... They were professional murderers'. For another tribute to the dead by Housman, see his short elegy 'Here Dead We Lie' in *Up the Line to Death*, p. 149.

QUESTION
Could the last two lines be read as offering some hope – that even in wartime the grass continues to grow?

QUESTION

What is the effect of the two short questions 'passengers ask the conductor' in lines 8 and 9?

GLOSSARY

1	**Austerlitz** battle in 1805 when Napoleon defeated Austria and Russia
1	**Waterloo** battle in 1815 that brought about Napoleon's final defeat
4	**Gettysberg** victory by the Union army in the American Civil War in 1863, with about 50,000 casualties
5	**Ypres** Belgian town where battles were fought in 1914, 1915 and 1917, with over 600,000 casualties
5	**Verdun** French town, site of fighting throughout most of 1916, resulting in about 800,000 casualties

ROBERT FROST: RANGE-FINDING

- A cobweb in No Man's Land is cut by a bullet. After the disturbance, the creatures continue their lives.

During 'range-finding' (testing the distance a bullet travels on the battlefield) a bullet severs a thread in a cobweb and cuts a flower. A bird continues to visit its nest nearby and a butterfly, after a brief hesitation, settles on the broken flower. The spider, annoyed that the trembling of the web did not mean a fly had been caught, returns to its hiding place.

COMMENTARY

The apparent lack of incident in this **sonnet** is the point. Frost implies that nature carries on, adjusting to the minor disturbance of a passing bullet with only a brief hesitation. To birds, butterflies and spiders the battle (mentioned only in line 1) is a matter of indifference. The human significance of the bullet is mentioned only in passing, as if of little importance: 'before it stained a single human breast' (3). Although the tiny creatures might seem far more vulnerable than humans, their tranquillity is hardly touched by the bullet which brings death to soldiers. There is a sense of stillness to the scene, reinforced by Frost's careful choice of words: the cobweb is 'diamond-strung' (1); there are 'straining cables wet with silver dew' (11); the butterfly's fragility is emphasised by its 'fluttering' (8). The sonnet ends on a note of anti-climax as the spider discovers the disturbance was not caused by a trapped insect; 'sullenly' attributes feeling to the spider – and, by implication, suggests that nature regards the intrusion of war with hostility, undergoing its own test of endurance. This is indeed 'No Man's Land'.

Structurally the sonnet repeats in the **sestet** a description of the event mentioned in the **octave**, this time with the focus on the spider rather than the flower. The awkwardness of the three lines describing the butterfly (6–8), in which the reader needs to work out the syntax of the first line ('A butterfly [that the flower's] fall had dispossessed' – that is, that had been dislodged from the flower where it was resting) means that a reading ought to mimic the insect's uncertain, hesitant movements. This is emphasised by the longer, eleven-syllable line 8 with the inversion of the normal word order at the end: 'fluttering clung'.

CONTEXT

According to a letter by Frost, he saved this poem only because his friend Edward Thomas (see pp. 179–80) 'thought it so good a description of No Man's Land' (*Selected Letters of Robert Frost*, ed. Lawrence Thompson). It was first published in 1916.

GLOSSARY

10   **mullein** tall plant with spiky yellow flowers

GUILLAUME APOLLINAIRE: CALLIGRAM, 15 MAY 1915

- The poem describes, in words and by its shape, the night sky over the soldier-poet's position.

The soldier-poet describes the dark of the night sky over his gun battery; a shell passes over; the evening star shines down on him.

COMMENTARY

Apollinaire's **shape-poem**, one of two short poems in *The Oxford Book of War Poetry* translated from French, is a kind of snapshot or rapid sketch of a moment at the Front at night. Like calligraphy, on which the term *calligram* is based, the appearance of the words is important. The first two **couplets** seem conventional enough, but

CHECK THE POEM

The other poem translated from French is 'Little Song of the Maimed' by Benjamin Péret, a surrealist like Apollinaire, who also served in the French army (p. 171).

CONTEXT

Guillaume Apollinaire wrote in a letter to André Billy: 'The *Calligrammes* are an idealisation of **free verse** poetry and typographical precision in an era when typography is reaching a brilliant end to its career, at the dawn of the new means of reproduction that are the cinema and the phonograph.' The soldier-poet Apollinaire is credited with inventing the term surrealism in 1917.

then the words form themselves into the shapes of a star and a cannon. Three of the couplets also rely on **similes** to create their impression. Appropriately, the sky is like 'ink' (1) – the poem, of course, is made legible by the use of ink – though Apollinaire puzzles the reader by making it both 'blue and black' (1) and then by saying his eyes 'drown' (2) as if in a sea. This alerts us to the **surreal** elements in the poem. To Apollinaire (as to many others in all branches of the arts), the war brought such strange and contradictory experiences that artists were able only to record their impressions rather than attempt to make any sense of them. The second **stanza** illustrates this further: without punctuation (the whole poem has none) he records the darkness, a shell and himself – leaving the reader to guess at his feelings. Nature provides beauty in the form of the star, which he compares, exotically, to a jewel in a crown and to the glance of a beautiful woman. The effect of these images of beauty, reinforced by the archaic phrasing 'lovely she' (7), is to complete the disjuncture between beauty and danger which Apollinaire felt at the front during the night.

GLOSSARY

title	**Calligram** words drawn into a visual image; the term was coined by Apollinaire for his volume-poems *Calligrammes*, subtitled *Poems of War and Peace 1913–1916*, first published in 1918
title	**15 May 1915** this was the first day of the Battle of Festubert, a British–Canadian–Indian action in support of the French
6	**rajah** Indian king or prince
8	**battery** group of heavy guns and their equipment

W. B. YEATS: EASTER 1916

- Yeats pays tribute to the leaders of the Easter Rising against British rule in Ireland which took place in April 1916.
- Their actions have transformed them into heroes and ensured them places of honour in the roll of Irish history.

The poet describes in the first stanza how he had, in the past, met the rebel leaders and exchanged pleasantries with them but not taken them seriously. Their actions in the Easter Rising have completely changed his view of them; their actions are no longer 'casual comedy' (37). The second stanza describes them in turn; without naming them he attributes special qualities to each one. 'That woman' (17) was Constance, Countess Markiewicz, a revolutionary nationalist and suffragette who, like the others, was sentenced to death for her part in the Rising (this was commuted to life imprisonment 'on account of the prisoner's sex'). Coming from a wealthy landowning family in Ireland, she had spent her youth in such pursuits as riding with the hounds (23). 'This man' (24) was Patrick Pearse, poet (in both Gaelic and English) and founder of St Enda's School, who was president of the Provisional Government in Dublin in Easter week. '[H]is helper and friend' (26) was Thomas MacDonagh, another poet and critic. 'This other man' (31) was John MacBride, who had married Maude Gonne, the woman Yeats had loved for many years – the 'bitter wrong' (33) was his ill-treatment of his wife. Each of them has been '[t]ransformed utterly' (39) by their actions and subsequent death.

The third stanza seems to be digression, with its descriptions of a horse crossing a stream, the clouds shifting across the sky and the call of the water-fowl. The word 'stone' in lines 43 and 56 link this to Yeats's theme, that devotion to a cause, in this case Irish nationalism (and in particular the battle over the Home Rule Bill, which was shelved when war broke out in 1914), can turn hearts from life and love into a coldness. This was hinted back in line 20, when the 'woman's ... voice grew shrill' with political argument, and picked up at the start of the final stanza, where 'Too long a sacrifice / Can make a stone of the heart' (57–8). Yeats now brings his argument together: only 'Heaven' knows when the sacrifices (of those who died and, we assume, those who will follow them) will be enough. 'England may keep faith' (68) with the promises made to reward the Irish for support during the First World War. Our role, he says, is to commemorate them alongside earlier heroes of Irish history, so for the first time he names four of them at the end of the poem, adding Patrick Connolly (a trade union

CONTEXT

In all, sixteen men were shot for their part in the Easter Rising, as Yeats commemorates in the next poem, 'Sixteen Dead Men' (p. 174), where again he refers to the list of Irish heroes, naming two figures who died in the Irish Rebellion of 1798, 'Lord Edward [FitzGerald] and Wolfe Tone' (16).

? QUESTION

What do you think Yeats means by the 'terrible beauty' that has been 'born' as a result of Easter 1916?

CHECK THE BOOK

The Irish playwright Sean O'Casey attacked the glorification of violence by the nationalist movement in plays such as *The Plough and the Stars* (1926). His play *The Silver Tassie* (1929) is a powerful indictment of the waste of the First World War, combining a realistic portrayal of the tragedy of sportsman Harry Heegan, whose life was destroyed by the war, with an expressionistic vision of the nightmare of the Front Line. It was rejected by W. B. Yeats and the managers of the Abbey Theatre in 1928; Yeats declared that it was 'all anti-war propaganda to the exclusion of plot and character'.

organiser and Commandant in the Dublin Post Office when it was seized and the Republic declared) to his earlier list.

COMMENTARY

The detailed account above might give the impression that the poem can be appreciated only with a good knowledge of Irish history and Yeats's own life. In fact it derives its power, at least for the modern reader, more from the simplicity of Yeats's form. The **allusions** to the characters who interested him most (he selects only four, one of them the husband of the woman he had loved for almost thirty years) and the description of a country stream in the third stanza could make it seem that Yeats is concerned only to wrestle with his personal feelings. In one sense this is true; Yeats is, amongst other things, describing a change of heart, which he hints at in his reference to the 'vivid faces' of the nationalist leaders (2) and the 'mocking tale' (10) he would previously tell to his friends; he had even attacked the new middle classes who 'fumble in a greasy till' in an earlier poem, 'September 1913', which lamented that 'romantic Ireland's dead and gone'. But this is more than a recantation, it is also an incantation. Yeats's simple three-beat **rhythm** and run-on lines propel the reader forward through the eighty lines, pausing three times on a variation of lines 15 and 16, with the emphasis on 'utterly' and the **oxymoronic** 'terrible beauty' of the rising. The *abab* **rhyme** (sometimes disguised by **half-rhymes**, as in lines 2 and 4) adds to this sense of urgency, so that despite the careful construction the whole poem has a conversational tone. The third **stanza** controls this by introducing a more thoughtful note, in which Yeats perhaps gives a clue about another kind of 'beauty', that of the Irish countryside whose freedom the rebels sought. Here too there is a sense of change in repetition: 'cloud to tumbling cloud' (47). Yeats does not resolve the conflict between hearts of 'stone' and the vitality of life; he implies that history will do that, though only by a series of unanswered questions in the final stanza.

It might seem **ironic** that Yeats had earlier refused to write a 'war poem', as he writes in 'On Being Asked for a War Poem' (p. 171). It was not just the dramatic nature of the events in 1916 that changed his mind; Yeats was an Irish nationalist who did not share the patriotic fervour that swept England in 1914, when Ireland was more concerned about Home Rule and the associated risk of a Protestant rebellion in Ulster.

GLOSSARY		
14	**motley**	jester's multicoloured costume
23	**harriers**	hunting dogs
25	**wingèd horse**	Pegasus, a creature in Greek mythology and here used as a symbol of poetic inspiration
78	**green**	the colour of the Irish nationalist flag and the symbol of Irish Republicanism

W. B. Yeats: An Irish Airman Foresees His Death

- An airman reflects on his fate; it is the joy of flight that has drawn him to the clouds.

An Irish airman – Major Robert Gregory, the only son of Yeats's close friend and supporter Lady Gregory, who was killed in 1918 – looks ahead to a forthcoming flight and anticipates his possible death in the air. He states that he neither hates the Germans nor loves those he protects (at the time of his death Gregory was in Italy but the reference is clearly to the English) since his 'countrymen' (6) are from Kiltartan, an area in County Galway in Ireland whose lives will be unchanged whatever happens to him. Nor is he flying out of duty or in pursuit of glory – only because of the 'impulse of delight' (11). Compared to this, everything else seems insignificant.

COMMENTARY

'Balance' appears twice in the poem, as a verb (13) and as a noun (16), and the whole poem reads like an exercise that evokes the delicate balance of forces that enables the airman's plane to stay aloft. The lines are mostly paired, either running on like the first two or echoing and balancing each other as lines 3 and 4 do. The rhymes are balanced in pairs, *abab*, to link each pair of lines, and the

CHECK THE BOOK

Sebastian Barry's *A Long Long Way* (2005) tells the story of Willy Dunne, an Irish volunteer in the British Army who finds himself caught up in the Easter Rising when he returns home to Dublin on leave. The novel portrays the confusion and pain caused by the divided loyalties of the central character both in Ireland and on the Western Front. See also Frank McGuinness's play *Observe the Sons of Ulster Marching Towards the Somme* (1986), about eight Protestants from the 36th Ulster Division, most of whom are killed on the first day of the battle.

CHECK THE POEM

'An Irish Airman Foresees His Death' should be read in conjunction with 'Reprisals', which Yeats wrote in 1920 (p. 175). Yeats imagines Major Gregory's spirit returning to Kiltartan Cross where 'Half-drunk or whole-mad soldiery [the Royal Irish Constabulary or "Black and Tans"] / Are murdering your tenants there'. In an **ironic parody** of line 9 of his earlier poem, Yeats writes: 'Nor law nor parliament take heed' and describes Gregory as lying 'among the other cheated dead'.

poem also turns around its centre point, with the last eight lines answering the first eight by explaining why he flies. At times Yeats resorts to repetition to emphasise his points, as in lines 3 to 6, where he changes only two words in each couplet, balancing 'fight' and 'hate' with 'guard' and 'love', for example. In lines 9 and 10 he uses 'nor' repeatedly to stress the reasons he is not fighting (such as duty and the quest for honour that Brooke, Asquith and others wrote about). Yeats uses the **rhetorical** device of **chiasmus**, where two phrases are related to each other through a reversal in the word order for greater effect. This can be seen in lines 14 and 15, which suggest the centrality of the present moment: 'The years to come seemed *waste of breath*, / A *waste of breath* the years behind'. Yeats also makes use of the **caesura** to emphasise this weighing of options; in line 13 the line breaks clearly, repeating the same idea in the second half. The last line moves the break further towards the end of the line, to make 'this death' (itself balancing 'this life') more a climax, more certain and more final. The cumulative effect of this repetition and revision is both powerful and memorable, suggesting a mind calmly and deliberately taking a fateful course.

Siegfried Sassoon: The Hero

- An officer visits a dead soldier's mother to tell her how he died.
- She is proud of her son's supposed gallantry, though in truth 'Jack' was a coward and the officer has lied to her.

The poem describes a visit by an officer to deliver a letter from the Colonel about her son who has just died. Outside the house, the officer reflects on the 'gallant lies' (8) that he has just told her and on the unpleasant truth of the soldier's cowardice and attempts to get away from the front line. Now only Jack's mother cares for his memory.

Commentary

The poem replays a small drama, doubtless painfully familiar to many families: the arrival of a comrade to tell a parent about a soldier's death. Sassoon puts in the mother's mouth some platitudes: 'as he'd have wished' (1) and 'We mothers are so proud' (5). The **pathos** of the situation is emphasised by the **enjambement** of lines 3 and 4, mimicking the breaking of her 'tired voice' as she is overcome with emotion. This scene is promptly undercut by the patronising tone adopted by the officer in the second **stanza**: the mother is now a 'poor old dear' (8) whose 'gentle triumph' (11) is based on falsehood. In line 9, Sassoon says she will 'nourish' these lies 'all her days' – where we might expect the words to sustain her, he implies that she will instead feed them by recalling and perhaps embellishing them so that (though she is unaware of the deception) the lies will grow. The words 'her glorious boy' (12) suggest how this might be: these seem to be her words rather than those of the officer. The third stanza completes the shift in tone, with brutal terms such as 'cold-footed, useless swine' included in the description of 'Jack's' cowardice under fire (13). The final **couplet** is more thoughtful; the soldier, coward or not, has been 'blown to small bits' and now no one cares – except his mother. The 'poor old dear' of line 8 is now described more sympathetically as 'that lonely woman with white hair'.

Structurally the poem follows a straightforward plan for each section of the **narrative**. The first and third six-line stanzas rhyme *aabb*, giving the impression, at least in the first stanza, that the mother's words are platitudes. The middle stanza adopts an *abab* rhyme scheme, perhaps to suggest the change to the officer's voice and more reflective tone. The poem ends with a couplet focusing on the mother, whose loneliness seems to be emphasised by the run-on last line and a half, with the contrast between 'no one' and 'except that lonely woman'.

CHECK THE POEM

For more of Sassoon's views on the ways civilians viewed the sacrifices of soldiers, see 'They' (p. 176), where the Bishop is portrayed as talking foolishly about 'a just cause' and daring death. In his 'To Any Dead Officer' (*Up the Line to Death*, p. 97) he addresses an imagined officer: 'you were all out to try and save your skin' but, like 'Jack', he died just the same. Sassoon wrote of these poems: 'These performances had the quality of satirical drawings. They were very deliberately written to disturb complacency.'

GLOSSARY		
13	cold-footed	cowardly
15	Wicked Corner	trenches were designed with frequent corners to prevent enemy fire along the full length of the trench if it was overrun; features were given names and this one implies the place was dangerous

CHECK THE BOOK

Sassoon describes the incident which formed the basis for this poem in Part Eight (section V) of his *Memoirs of an Infantry Officer*, first published in 1930. After finding the body, he comments: 'Stumbling on, I could only mutter to myself that this was really a bit too thick. (That, however, was an exaggeration; there is nothing remarkable about a dead body in a European War, or a squashed beetle in a cellar.)' (Faber, 2000, p. 163).

CHECK THE POEM

How does this poem compare with Sassoon's 'Everyone Sang' (p. 178), which describes a moment when the 'horror / Drifted away'?

- A soldier, stumbling along a captured trench in the dark, sees what he thinks is a sleeping soldier and demands to be given directions.
- The man is dead; in horror, the soldier staggers up to the surface.

The poem describes an incident following the capture of German trenches. The soldier is trying to find his way back to headquarters along an unfamiliar, and apparently deserted, system of tunnels fifty feet underground. By the light of his torch he can make out only vague shapes. He trips over a body under a rug and, taking it for a sleeping soldier, pulls his arm in an attempt to wake him. When this fails, his own lack of sleep causes him to lose patience; he curses the man and kicks him. But when his torch beam falls on the face, he realises the man has died in 'agony' (17) ten days ago, with his fingers still grasping the fatal wound. In horror, the soldier staggers on till he sees daylight and climbs to the surface, where the battle continues.

COMMENTARY

Sassoon's account has a nightmarish quality, in which the soldier seems to have no understanding of or control over events. The verbs convey the uncertainty and threatening nature of the situation: 'groping' (1), 'sniffed' (3), 'tripping', 'grabbed' (8), 'staggered' (19). This effectively suggests the danger; in unfamiliar territory, the enemy could be round the next corner and he tells us that 'the rosy gloom of battle' is 'overhead' (7). The irregular construction of the **stanzas** (no two are the same length) adds to the impression of confusion, as does the jumble of items listed, staccato fashion, in lines 4 and 5: 'Tins, boxes, bottles, shapes too vague to know'. The **rhymes**, however, do contribute to unifying the whole poem; 'sleep' in the third stanza rhymes with 'heap' at the beginning of the fourth, and 'wound' in the last line of stanza 4 is echoed in (though not quite rhymed with) 'found' in the first line of the final stanza. There are other links, too: 'step by step' in the opening line appears again in the last line, and 'the unwholesome air' of line 3 becomes 'the twilight air' in line 24.

The use of two verbs in the first three words gives a sudden jolt to the start of the third stanza. The soldier's angry words receive 'No reply' (11), adding to the chilling effect. The fourth stanza also starts with a single word marked off by a comma: 'Savage' (14). The vocabulary used to describe the contrast between the 'soft, unanswering heap' and the reality of the corpse is particularly brutal; 'livid', 'terribly glaring', 'agony', 'clutched' and 'blackening' (16–18). The haunting effects continue in the final stanza, where he is still 'Alone'; Sassoon describes 'Dawn's ghost' (the pale imitation, it implies, of real daylight) and the 'muttering creatures underground' who seem to be spectres (21) living in 'hell' (25). No wonder he has 'sweat of horror in his hair' (23). The final line conveys the return of some kind of calm, with his climb suggested by the **alliterative** repetition of 'step by step' bringing him to the surface – though he has reminded us that there is danger here, too, with the 'boom of shells' mentioned in line 22.

GLOSSARY

title	**Rear-Guard** a group of soldiers who protect the rear of an army
title	**Hindenburg Line** a fortified system of German defences in north-eastern France
12	**neck** slang term for cheek, rudeness

SIEGFRIED SASSOON: THE GENERAL

- The General seemed a cheerful character when the soldiers saw him on their way to battle but his incompetent planning led to the deaths of most of them.

The General had greeted the soldiers cheerfully on the way to the front line – now most of them are dead because of the incompetence of him and his staff. He had made a good impression on Harry at

 CHECK THE POEM
Compare this poem with Robert Graves's 'Sergeant-Major Money' (p. 195), which features 'a batty major, and [a] Colonel, who drank'.

CONTEXT

Arras (line 6) is a French town near the front line where a series of battles was fought; in 1917, when this poem is dated in Sassoon's manuscript, there was a large offensive from 9 April to 16 May which resulted in heavy casualties. Amongst them, on the first day, was the poet Edward Thomas (see pp. 179–80).

the time but now both he and his friend Jack are dead thanks to the General's plan.

COMMENTARY

This is one of Sassoon's bitterly **satirical** poems in which the young suffer because of the folly of the old. The hearty cheerfulness of the General, emphasised by his repeated greeting at the start of the poem, is undercut by the telling use at the end of line 3 of the word 'dead'. The lot of the common soldier, whose language Sassoon imitates in the abbreviation ''em' (3) and in 'cheery old card' (5), is made clear by the words 'slogged … with rifle and pack' (6). Sassoon uses **rhyme** (see 'They', p. 176) to stress the satire, linking what 'the General said' (1) with the men: 'dead' (3). The final three lines, though separated by a line of asterisks in Sassoon's manuscript, all rhyme, with the savagery reaching a climax with the final 'plan of attack'. What use, the poet implies, are 'Harry and Jack' or 'rifle and pack' if the planning is by 'incompetent swine' (4), however cheerful?

SIEGFRIED SASSOON: GLORY OF WOMEN

- Sassoon comments that women love soldiers as heroes and they delight in war stories; they have no appreciation of the horrors of war.
- A German mother also has no idea of the fate of her son.

This poem describes how women love soldiers at home on leave or wounded (in mentionable parts of the body) and are impressed by medals. They work in munitions factories and are thrilled by tales of heroism. They see war as glorious and have no idea of its hellish nature. In reality, whilst a German mother knits socks for her son, his body is trampled underfoot in the battle.

COMMENTARY

This **sonnet** is another of Sassoon's attacks on those remote from the brutalities of battle. The title itself is **ironic**; it does not celebrate women but rather attacks them – or at least those who unthinkingly accept the falsehood that 'chivalry redeems the war's disgrace' (4). The repeated use of 'you' (eight times in all) makes the poem an accusation and a very personal one; by their hero-worship as well as by the shells they make, the women are supporting the war. The **alliteration** links their 'delight' with 'dirt and danger' (5–6). Sassoon places the verb 'thrilled' at the end of line 6 for emphasis, preceding it with 'fondly' to imply that these tales only increase the attractiveness of men in their eyes and thus encourages further fighting. Alliteration is used again to emphasise 'hell's last horror' (10), how the men, 'trampling the terrible corpses', are 'blind with blood' (11).

The final three lines, separated by the indentation, mark a sudden switch of focus from Sassoon's accusation to an address to the 'German mother' (12) whose son is trampled by the running British troops. Like her British counterparts, she is supporting the war but Sassoon's portrayal is **ambiguous**, as she is surely also a victim, just as her dead son has become. This change of emphasis to a more thoughtful mood is reflected in the way the hectic pace of the preceding two lines describing battle ('breaks ... run ... trampling', 10–11) gives way to a slower **rhythm**, with the final two lines run on as though the mother's knitting is viewed in the same image as the trampled corpse.

CHECK THE BOOK

Jon Stallworthy writes of this poem: 'Like many of Sassoon's later war poems, this is launched at the reader like a hand-grenade' (*Anthem for Doomed Youth*, Constable, 2002, p. 68).

? QUESTION

What do you think is the effect of making a woman a victim of the war (in the last three lines) as well as attacking women for their glorification of war?

GLOSSARY

8	laurelled	crowned with a laurel wreath as a sign of glory

EDWARD THOMAS: RAIN

- The poet lies awake listening to the rain, thinking of his own mortality and of all those he loves who may also be listening to it.

Lying awake at midnight in a 'bleak hut' (2), the poet is reminded of the certainty of his own death. He prays that none of those he loves hears the rain this night, either because they are dying or because, like him, they feel helpless in the face of death. It is as though the rain has washed everything away except the love of death.

COMMENTARY

Like all of Thomas's 'war poems', 'Rain' was written after he enlisted in July 1915 but before he sailed for France in January 1917. This poem is dated 7 January 1916 and the hut mentioned in the poem is presumably an army hut where Thomas was sleeping during training. However, as Jon Silkin explains in a detailed and sensitive exploration of this poem in Chapter 5 of *Out of Battle*, the poem has its origins in a passage in Thomas's prose work, *The Icknield Way* that dates from as early as 1911. The sense of despair is present in both. The rain prompts in the poet the thoughts of his death (3), perhaps because, coming in the middle of the night, it emphasises his 'solitude', a word which occurs in lines 2 and 6 and again, as 'solitary', in line 10. However, the war is also present here, though only by implication, as he prays 'that none whom once I loved / Is dying tonight' or 'in pain' (8–11). The image of 'Myriads of broken reeds all still and stiff' (14) suggests bodies on a battlefield; the rain reminds him that 'cold water' (13) cannot revive the dead reeds any more than lying awake 'in sympathy' (11) can help the dead and dying. 'Helpless', placed at the beginning of line 12, stresses the impotence of feeling, since it has no power in the face of death.

Thomas brings the poem to a conclusion by referring again to the rain which has been a constant note during the poem; now it is a 'tempest' (18) of such power that it has 'dissolved' all other human feelings 'except the love of death' (16). Earlier, he has used a blessing, though one of a rather strange, unsettling kind: 'Blessed are the dead that the rain rains upon' (7) is an echo of the Beatitudes in the Sermon on the Mount ('Blessed are those who mourn', Matthew 5:4), but a bleak blessing the tone of which recurs in the last four lines. Thomas's language is tentative and subtle: 'what is perfect' is death, but he does not tell the reader why, nor why he feels unsure whether it is love he feels for it (17). The final line is qualified by the words in parenthesis: 'the tempest tells me', which leaves the force of his conclusion divided between the first and last words of the line. Does he accept what the tempest says, that death

CHECK THE NET

As well as extracts in Silkin's *Out of Battle*, you can read both Thomas's poem and the prose passage from *The Icknield Way* on Cambridge University's Converse site. Go to the A Level seminars area and look for the past seminar called 'Inspiration and Recollection', **http://aspirations. english.cam.ac.uk** 'cannot disappoint'? The reader is left unsure, but it is a further, chilling, reminder of mortality that had first occurred in the third line. This care to balance and elaborate on what he is saying is an indication that although Thomas uses an apparently casual **free-verse** style, the poem achieves its effects by means of careful patterning, repetition and qualification in which innocuous words such as 'but', 'neither' and 'if' play an important part.

GLOSSARY

14	**Myriads** a very large number

IVOR GURNEY: TO HIS LOVE

- The poem is an elegy for a fellow-soldier, and is addressed to the dead soldier's 'love'.
- It asks that his body be covered with flowers from the banks of his native River Severn.

The poem laments the loss of a soldier who would seem, like Gurney, to have served in the Gloucester Regiment. No longer will the soldiers be able to be together in the Cotswolds or on the River Severn. He asks for the body to be covered with 'masses' (18) of flowers from the Severn to hide the fatal wound.

COMMENTARY

In four **stanzas**, Gurney moves from a personal lament that recalls his beloved Gloucestershire, through pride in the soldier's sacrifice, to final horror at the bleeding, dying body. After the simple statement, 'He's gone' (1), the poem describes the activities the friends had shared. Walking in the countryside and boating on the river are portrayed in terms reminiscent of **pastoral** poetry, far removed from battle. The terse lines in the second stanza seem to suggest the energy of the man rowing on the river: the highly stressed 'Is not as you' (7) is matched by 'Under the blue' (9, forcing the reader to suggest a missing word such as 'sky') as if the quick

CHECK THE FILM

The BBC's excellent documentary series *The Great War* (1984), now available on DVD, makes extensive use of archive materials and interviews with veterans.

CHECK THE POEM
You can see a reproduction of Gurney's manuscript for 'To His Love' in Jon Stallworthy's *Anthem for Doomed Youth* (Constable, 2002, p. 157). According to Stallworthy, the subject of the poem was F. W. Harvey who was, it transpired, not killed but taken prisoner.

oar strokes are 'driving' the boat that shoots forward in the longer line 10. This is reinforced by the way that each of these lines (second, fourth and fifth) rhymes.

The third **stanza** hints at the body's disfigurement before moving to more conventional pride in the sacrifice by using the word 'nobly' (13) and 'violets of pride' (14). This suggests a conventional, patriotic tribute to the fallen hero, but the urgency of the first line of the final stanza alters the mood. 'Masses of memoried flowers' are needed (18) because the body has become, it is implied, so hideously disfigured. The raw emotion of the last two lines, in which the wound is left disturbingly vague and yet horrific by the use of the words 'red wet / Thing', tell us that the poet, despite what he says, cannot 'forget'. Dividing the three words in this way is powerful: the simple two words, both stressed syllables, at the end of line 19 convey the rawness of the wound and make the reader pause fractionally before the word 'thing' placed at the beginning of the final line, as if the poet cannot bear to name what he has seen.

> ## GLOSSARY
>
> | 3 | **Cotswold** the Cotswolds is a range of hills in south-west England, mainly in Gurney's native Gloucestershire |
> |---|---|

IVOR GURNEY: BALLAD OF THE THREE SPECTRES

- A soldier meets three apparitions who foretell different futures for him: to be wounded and sent home, to die or to live until the last days of the war and die in an 'hour of agony'.

As a soldier marches through mud he is met by three mocking ghosts who taunt him with visions of the future. The first says he will be wounded, and pleased to be sent home to recuperate. The second foretells his death in the freezing mud. The final ghost curses him to live until the last hours of the war only to endure agony. The soldier survives but waits to see if the third spectre's prophecy will come true.

COMMENTARY

Gurney uses the traditional **ballad** form to powerful effect in a poem that deals with any soldier's constant preoccupation in wartime: the prospects of survival. Behind the seemingly artless use of simple four-line stanzas lies a carefully crafted **rhyme** scheme that helps create the haunted atmosphere of the poem. The second and fourth lines of each stanza use the same 'ee' sound as rhyme. This ties together the taunting, tantalising visions the spectres hold up before the weary soldier, from the comforting 'Blighty' (8) through the certainty of death in Picardy (12) to the unspecified 'agony' of line 16. His final word, 'verity', an archaic term, is a reminder of the ballad form's historical roots; Gurney has also used the old word 'fleering' in line 3. The harsh realities of modern warfare are made clear, however, in the second line's reference to 'mud' and the prospect of freezing to death in line 11. The jaunty **rhythm** and informal, conversational style (such as 'a right brave soldier', 5) recall the traditional form but this is undercut by the macabre vision of the spectres and their prophecies which are more like curses, as line 14 makes clear. The poem ends with the soldier still alive – but even his drill, counted off 'by one–two–three' (18), is a reminder of the fateful spectres.

<table>
<tr><td colspan="2">**GLOSSARY**</td></tr>
<tr><td>1</td><td>**Ovillers** a village in northern France, the site of heavy fighting during the Battle of the Somme</td></tr>
<tr><td>3</td><td>**fleering** laughing in contempt</td></tr>
<tr><td>8</td><td>**Blighty** soldiers' slang for home or England; 'a nice Blighty' was a wound that resulted in the soldier being sent home</td></tr>
<tr><td>12</td><td>**Picardie** an area in northern France (in English often spelt Picardy)</td></tr>
</table>

CONTEXT

Ivor Gurney's own fate is in some ways reflected in this poem. Wounded in April 1917, he recovered but was then gassed in August and sent home to convalesce. He had a breakdown and, in Edmund Blunden's words, 'passed though a period of exceptional misery' (John Silkin, *Out of Battle* (Routledge, 1987), p. 122). Although he recovered, the respite was only temporary and he spent the last fifteen years of his life, from 1922, confined to an asylum.

IVOR GURNEY: THE SILENT ONE

- During an attack one officer is killed crossing the barbed wire whilst the private lies flat.
- A second officer asks the private to crawl through a gap, but he refuses until he retreats and then comes back to the same place.

The soldier, part of a raiding party, describes how an officer is killed attempting to step over the wires and his body left hanging. Anxious to avoid death, the soldier keeps down under the wires; when another officer tells him to crawl through he politely refuses. After a while lying there under fire, they retreat, then return – to face the wires again.

COMMENTARY

Gurney's apparently shapeless poem captures a nightmarish incident in all its chaos. From the beginning it is fragmented, as if in the middle of a sentence. The reader has to work out that the 'who' of lines 1 and 2 is the officer – presumably the soldier is the other 'of two'. (Gurney was himself a private soldier, not an officer.) The disjointed sentence describes the officer's death; by contrast with the 'infinite lovely chatter' (3), this death is horrible, leaving his body suspended on the barbed wire whilst his companion, fearful for his own life, takes cover. There is affection not only for his familiar accent, reminding the soldier of home, but even for his folly in attempting to step over the wire; Gurney describes him as 'a noble fool' (5), but he 'ended' (again, Gurney seems to miss out words such as 'his life'). Unlike the officer, it seems, the soldier is more concerned to survive and keep 'unshaken' (8). The second officer, urging him forward to risk a similar fate, is also described by his voice: it is an unappealing 'finicking accent' (9). The repeated negatives of the next sentence emphasise the absurd nature of the command: 'There was no hole no way to be seen, / Nothing but chance of death' (12–13). The grim reality of what faces him is spelt out, as if catching the very moment a bullet strikes (perhaps recalling the wounds on the body hanging on the wires in front of him): 'death, after tearing of clothes' (13). The situation is

CONTEXT

That the soldier 'Thought of music' (15) is a reminder that Ivor Gurney was an accomplished musician who studied at the Royal College of Music before the war. As a composer he is particularly admired for his song settings.

unresolved; the soldier lies trying to keep sane by thinking of music. His 'deep oaths' to God (15) are, like his words to the officer, polite yet there is an underlying anger in the poem. There is a great deal of repetition and it reaches its climax in the final line as, having retreated, he goes forward once more to face 'the screen' of the wires and, it is implied, the body still hanging there.

GLOSSARY	
3	**Bucks** Buckinghamshire
5	**stripes** stripes on a uniform that indicate the wearer is an officer

ISAAC ROSENBERG: DEAD MAN'S DUMP

- Wagons run over some dead bodies on their way to the front.
- The poet reflects on the fate of these men.

Soldiers are carrying wire to the front line on gun carriages. On the way their wheels run over the bodies of the dead. The poet reflects on the fate that has brought them to this cruel end. Where are their souls now? Some have only just died; he describes how one man's brains are 'splattered' (48) onto the stretcher-bearer's face, while another dies just as the wagons come round the corner and roll over him.

COMMENTARY

The brutality of the scene Rosenberg describes is clear in the title: the men are being abandoned like so much rubbish that the unheeding gun carriages roll over. There is little action in the poem, just a few lurid snapshots. Beginning with the wagons laden with wire lurching to the front – their disturbing movement concisely evoked by the word 'plunging' (1) – he describes a wounded soldier who, it seems, was hit by a shell, killed and left with the others in the 'dump'. The poet imagines him longing for help – but all that comes are the cruel wheels of the carriages that 'grazed his dead face' (79). The poem's central concern is what has happened, and is

CONTEXT

In a letter to Edward Marsh dated 8 May 1917, Rosenberg wrote: 'I've written some lines suggested by going out wiring, or rather carrying wire up the line on limbers and running over dead bodies lying about' (John Silkin, *Out of Battle*, Routledge, 1987, p. 281). You can see a reproduction of his corrected typescript for the poem, dated 'May 14 1917', in Jon Stallworthy's *Anthem for Doomed Youth* (Constable, 2002, p. 175).

CHECK THE BOOK

There is an extended commentary on 'Dead Man's Dump' in Chapter 10 of John Silkin's *Out of Battle* (Routledge, 1987). Silkin writes: 'What Rosenberg does is to present a number of complex responses to combat, and then unify them into a single realization of how war entails one damaging, continuous impact on the body and the mind' (p. 281).

CHECK THE POEM

Compare Rosenberg's questions about life and death in 'Dead Man's Dump' with those in Owen's 'Futility' (p. 193).

happening, to the living and the dead in this place of desolation. Religious **imagery** is invoked in the first **stanza**, where the rolls of wire are compared to 'crowns of thorns' (3): as Christ was mocked by being made to wear a crown of thorns before his crucifixion, this wire will torment those who come into contact with it. In the first instance this will be the enemy, described as 'brutish men' (5), though a few lines later he makes it clear that the dead they run over are all the same: 'friend and foeman / Man born of man, and born of woman' (10–11). (There is a further suggestion of Christ's death in line 55, where the dead man is 'stretched at the cross roads'.)

The description of the wagon's progress is made sickening by the verbs 'lurched' (7) and 'crunched' (8). Despite the statement that this 'pained them not' (8) it is impossible not to see the corpses as human, for Rosenberg chooses words suggesting suffering, such as 'moan' and 'huddled' – even the shells are 'crying over them' (9–12). The next three stanzas question what has happened to these men and why they have died; 'Earth has waited for them' (14) but where have their souls gone? His response is to imagine the souls 'flung on your hard back' (23) as if no one cared. The answer to the repeated question, 'Who hurled them out?' (26), isn't given, though the accusation seems to be directed at humanity, the 'man born of man' of line 11. Now all their vitality, imagined in its sweetness as 'the wild honey of their youth' (31) has been snatched by the bullet, graphically described as a 'swift iron burning bee' (30) – the natural image made cruel by machinery. The living – including the **narrator** – are also threatened; they may feel 'immortal' but in fact they too seem fated for death, since they are 'flung on the shrieking pyre', an image picked up as he imagines the 'flames' of the funeral pyre 'beat loud on us' (32–6), just as the newly dead 'strode time with vigorous life' (43) a few minutes ago.

The poem's complex responses contain both brutality and 'human tenderness' (53), though the description undercuts that by pointing out that the stretcher-bearer's concern for the dying man is useless. So the bodies decay, with less life than the grass around them, their souls having only 'weak hands' (64). The vision is one of despair, in which the man's soul longs for 'light' (66) but the wheels come close only to graze his dead face. The references in the tenth stanza have an apocalyptic feel: 'the end' and 'the tide of the world' hint that this might be the end of all things.

GLOSSARY

1	**limbers** two-wheeled vehicles used to pull field guns; line 73 indicates they were pulled here by mules
32	**pyre** pile of wood heaped for burning a dead body
34	**ichor** the fluid said, in Greek mythology, to flow in the veins of the gods in place of blood

---

ISAAC ROSENBERG: RETURNING, WE HEAR THE LARKS

- Soldiers returning to camp at night are delighted by the songs of unseen larks.

In this poem, men making their way back to camp after dark are surprised to hear larks singing above them. The music gives them unexpected joy amidst the dangers that surround them.

COMMENTARY

This short poem is marked by a sense of danger, so that even the apparently innocent beauty of the larks' songs hides a threat – such is the effect of war on everything that touches the soldiers. The first word, 'Sombre', sets the tone and this is continued in the first two stanzas with words such as 'anguished' and 'poison-blasted'. Even rest is only 'a little safe sleep' (6), with perhaps a hint of the sleep of death. So although the larks bring 'strange joy' (7), it is in the context of night where 'Death could drop from the dark / As easily as song' (10–11). At best, Rosenberg implies, the 'music showering our upturned list'ning faces' (9) brings only temporary joy. Like the **Romantic** poet Shelley, Rosenberg attempts to describe the effect of the unexpected music on his feelings by means of **similes**. These are all tinged with threats; the blind man and the girl may be unaware but danger is near, unseen. The images are capable of multiple interpretations. Does the blind man (line 13) dream happily, lulled

CHECK THE POEM
The poem has echoes of 'To a Skylark' by Shelley (1792–1822), who writes of the lark in terms similar to line 9: 'from thy presence showers a rain of melody'.

CHECK THE POEM

An interesting comparison with Rosenberg's poem is 'The Lark Above the Trenches' by Muriel Graham (page 42 of *Scars Upon My Heart*). Although she also acknowledges the imminence of death, Graham writes that with the lark's song 'life soared triumphant'.

CONTEXT

Owen showed Sassoon the first draft of this poem when he met him at Craiglockhart War Hospital in 1917. Sassoon suggested a number of significant changes, which can be seen in the reproductions of the manuscripts in Chapter 8 of Stallworthy's *Wilfred Owen: A Biography* (Oxford, 1974). This important stage in Owen's development as a poet forms the basis of Stephen MacDonald's play, *Not About Heroes* (1982).

by the sea, or fearful of its danger? How conscious is the girl of the temptations she represents? The effect is unsettling.

The poem's irregular structure reflects this, with its shift between short lines with a suggestion of menace (such as the first and fourteenth lines) and longer ones. Lines 4 and 5 convey in their awkward **rhythm** the effort required to move the 'anguished limbs' whilst the third stanza captures in its repetition of sound and stress the song of the larks. **Rhyme** is deployed sparingly; in the final stanza, the 'dangerous tides' are linked to 'where a serpent hides' to emphasise the hidden perils.

WILFRED OWEN: ANTHEM FOR DOOMED YOUTH

- The poet asks what ceremonies will commemorate those who die in battle.
- Rather than religious ceremonies they will have the sounds of battle and the mourning of those grieving at home.

The **sonnet** asks two questions about the commemoration of the men who die in battle. The **octet** states that they will have only the sounds of battle itself as music to accompany their funerals. The **sestet** explains that instead of church candles, the sorrow of children will commemorate them and they will be held in the minds of those who love them.

COMMENTARY

Stallworthy suggests in his biography that in this poem Owen was responding with hostility to the Prefatory Note of the popular anthology *Poems of Today*, published in 1915 by the English Association (and reprinted many times since). The anonymous editor states that the aim is that 'boys and girls ... may also know something of the newer poetry of their day'. Referring to one (that is, Rupert Brooke) 'who has gone singing to lay his life down for his country's cause', the preface also includes the terms 'bugle-call' and 'passing bell' that recur in Owen's poem.

The sonnet is a commemoration of those who die like 'cattle' in the slaughterhouse (1), but it is an **ironic** counter to the religious ceremonies that Owen himself would have been familiar with from his time as an assistant to the Vicar of Dunsden. Those rituals he now characterises as 'mockeries' (5). Instead, the harsh sounds of battle will be their music and Owen echoes these in the **onomatopoeia** and **alliteration** of lines 3 and 4 in imitation of rifle-fire. The 'shrill, demented choirs of wailing shells' (7) continue this aural representation of the battlefield. A calmer note is sounded by the bugle in the final line of the octet – which by reminding us of the ceremony of the Last Post, sounded over a military funeral, slightly detracts from the picture Owen has created so far, since it is a more traditional commemoration of the fallen.

The bugle, sounded in 'sad shires' (8), has brought the mourning home and in the sestet Owen focuses on the 'boys and girls' whose loved ones have died. The brutality of the octet is here softened by references to 'candles', 'holy glimmers' and 'the pallor of girls' brows' (which, Owen says, in a play on words, 'shall be their pall', 9–12). The poem, always musical, slows in the final **couplet** to match the 'slow dusk' that is both literal and the darkness of death. The richness of Owen's vocabulary here indicates the continuing influence of **Romantic** poetry, particularly Keats (1795–1821), especially in the mellifluousness of the sestet. It is a style that can be heard to fade in his later poems as Owen strove for ways to represent the brutal realities of modern warfare.

www. CHECK THE NET
The manuscripts of Owen's drafts for this poem can be seen on the Oxford University First World War Poetry Digital Archive site in the tutorial 'An Introduction to Manuscript Studies', **www.ww1lit.com.** Find this section by clicking on 'Virtual Seminars'.

GLOSSARY

title	**Anthem**	song for a church choir, usually based on a passage in the Bible
1	**passing-bell**	church bell rung when someone has died
4	**orisons**	prayers (a word found in *Hamlet*, at the end of the famous 'To be or not to be' speech, when Hamlet sees Ophelia with a prayer-book)
12	**pall**	the cloth spread over a coffin at a funeral
14	**drawing-down of blinds**	it was customary to draw the blinds or close the curtains when a member of the household died

WILFRED OWEN: DULCE ET DECORUM EST

- Men returning from the lines are attacked by gas shells.
- One of them is too slow fitting his mask; they put him on a wagon and hear his agonised coughing as they follow.

A group of exhausted men are heading back from the front line when they come under attack from gas shells. They all manage to fit their protective helmets in time except one soldier who is caught and chokes on the poisonous fumes. The soldiers place him on a wagon and, following, hear and watch his suffering on the rough road. No one seeing this could claim that it was sweet to die for one's country.

COMMENTARY

This poem, written during the same period of intense creative activity at Craiglockhart Hospital that produced 'Anthem for Doomed Youth', is a passionate denunciation of the jingoistic writing that called young men nobly to offer themselves for the sake of their country. Where 'Anthem for Doomed Youth' (which was also written in response to patriotic sentiments) has a series of impressions of the angry music of battle, Owen here describes a single incident in horrific detail before turning to address those who would urge 'children' to seek 'desperate glory' (26). **Ironically** addressing the patriot as 'My friend' (25), Owen's view is clear: the children are being offered 'the old Lie' (27); the capital letter implies the status given to the sentiment.

The poem is written in sections of unequal length though with some skilful use of **rhyme**. The first **stanza** sets the scene, with the frequent use of **alliteration** stressing the anguish of weariness that the men feel, for example in the **simile**: 'like old beggars ... / Knock-kneed, coughing like hags' (1–2). Owen coins the word 'blood-shod' (6) to convey the state of the men's feet without boots, with its echo of 'bloodshed'. The short phrases break up the lines to suggest the limping progress of the men. Owen drops in the enemy shells, describing them as also being 'tired, outstripped', in the last

CONTEXT

The 'Five-Nine' (8) shells contained chlorine gas, a yellow-green cloud of vapour that, if inhaled, would within seconds destroy the victim's respiratory organs, bringing on choking attacks. It was first used by the Germans at the start of the second Battle of Ypres on 22 April 1915, when it caused the panic-stricken flight of French and Algerian troops. There is a graphic fictional account of this attack in Chapter 4 of Sebastian Barry's *A Long Long Way* (2005).

line. But the suggested pause between the stanzas is broken by the urgent cries of the men in the repeated single word, 'Gas!' (9), given capital letters the second time to convey the panic; their 'ecstasy' (9) is far from the usual sense of the word but perhaps suggests their relief as they manage to fit the gas masks. The man who was caught, however, is described in a succession of verbs in the present tense because, to the poet, he is still, now, 'stumbling ... drowning' (11–14). The nightmarish quality of this ever-present vision is conveyed by the isolation of the two lines beginning 'In all my dreams ...' (15). The verb 'plunges' suggests the desperation of the soldier, whilst the succession of 'guttering, choking, drowning' mimics both the sound and action of the scene.

The final stanza addresses the reader; although Owen's target, as line 25 eventually reveals, is anyone who tries to deceive the young with lies about 'glory' (26), his use of the second person 'you' in line 17 implicates everyone in the man's suffering. He makes sure we appreciate just how far from decorous this man's death is by the language of these lines, which form a single sentence of accumulating passion, including a series of **metaphors** and similes (as though the horror is so great that one comparison alone will not suffice). The climax in line 24 ends on 'innocent tongues' and is followed by a pause, indicated by the dash before the poet directly addresses the patriot in mocking terms as 'My friend'. The word 'innocent' is picked up in 'children' who (equally innocent and ignorant, it is implied) should not be lied to: the monosyllabic, equally stressed words 'The old Lie' (27) convey Owen's contempt for the Latin sentiment which ends the poem with a half-line, as if to stress it does not tell the truth.

 CHECK THE POEM
Early drafts of this poem contained the dedication 'To Jessie Pope etc' or 'To a certain Poetess'. Jessie Pope's jingoistic poem 'The Call' appeared in the *Daily Mail* on 26 November 1914. The poem appears in *Scars Upon My Heart*, p. 88; see **Themes: Patriotism** for a quotation from it.

GLOSSARY

title and line 28	**Dulce et decorum est / Pro patria mori** a quotation from one of the odes by the ancient Roman poet Horace which, Owen wrote to his mother, 'means of course *It is sweet and meet* to die for one's country. Sweet! and decorous!' You can see it in the original context on page 13 in *The Oxford Book of War Poetry*, where it appears in the fourth stanza of the first extract from Horace's Odes

continued

3	flares rockets sent up to burn brightly so that soldiers could see enemy activity at night
8	Five-Nines 5.9 inch (15 cm) artillery shells, in this case containing gas (which creates the 'thick green light' of line 13)
12	lime white chalky compound, sometimes called quicklime, which is caustic (causes burns)
16	guttering flickering like a candle flame about to go out, but also suggesting the guttural sound of the choking soldier

CONTEXT

The Planets, a 'Suite for Large Orchestra' by the English composer Gustav Holst, opens with the music of 'Mars, the Bringer of War'. Although the work was not performed until 1918, Holst apparently completed the music for 'Mars' in the summer of 1914, before the outbreak of the War. Like the music of Stravinsky's *Rite of Spring* (1913), which influenced his work, Holst's 'Mars' can thus be seen as ominously prophetic of the violence the War was about to unleash.

WILFRED OWEN: EXPOSURE

- A company of soldiers suffers the bitter cold of a night at the front.
- Dawn brings snow and a few bullets. They dream of spring in the countryside – but their lot is to lie out in the trenches.

The troops keep nervous watch during a bitterly cold night though, despite the distant sound of guns, 'nothing happens' (5, repeated three more times). They question why they are there. Dawn brings only gloomy relief; the enemy's bullets are less dangerous than the snow. In their dreams, they see a peaceful spring scene though it is one from which they are excluded. Their fate is, instead, to lie out in the trenches. Tonight, the cold will claim more lives. Still nothing happens.

COMMENTARY

The poem is a meditation on the purpose (or purposelessness) of war, conveyed through the thoughts and feelings of soldiers enduring the bitter cold on night duty at the front in the depths of winter. Stallworthy, in his biography of Owen, points out that Owen wrote the opening **stanzas** in reverse order. 'When, in the second draft, these two stanzas are transposed, the reader is led more logically across the salient to the whispering sentries and the wind in the wire' (*Wilfred Owen: A Biography*, p. 247). The

assonance and word-play of the opening line is typical of Owen's mature style, with the **sibilance** of 'merciless iced east winds' (1). He returns to this word-play on 'ice' in the final stanza, where 'all their eyes are ice' (39). The lack of activity is itself unsettling for the men, who 'keep awake because the night is silent' (2). The cruelty of war and nature combine to torment them as the wind, 'tugging on the wire' (6) whose barbs Owen mockingly calls 'brambles' (7), is compared to the 'agonies' of those who have died there as a result of man's inhumanity. The second stanza ends with the first of two questions: 'What are we doing here?' (10). Although this could be taken as a query about the point of their night's duty, it also implies a questioning of the purpose of the war itself. Like the question at the end of the fifth stanza, it is not answered, except, by implication, in the bleakness of the situation which Owen describes when he says in line 12: 'We only know war lasts, rain soaks, and clouds sag stormy.' For the men, war is as inevitable as the weather; beyond the brutal realities of their present situation, nothing is sure. In the kind of nature poetry which Owen evokes fleetingly in the sixth stanza, dawn would traditionally bring hope – instead, she brings 'poignant misery', a painful reminder of what might have been (11). Owen personifies dawn in a hostile, military image as an enemy, a 'melancholy army' (13) that 'attacks'. There is no welcoming bright glow of the rising sun, only 'shivering ranks of grey' (14); the snow clouds are **personified**, with a suggestion too of the grey uniforms worn by their other enemy, the German army.

The fifth stanza exemplifies a number of elements in Owen's style. The right **alliteration** on 'f' of the first line is combined with personification. The snow has already been described as 'deathly' (17), so the reader might wonder whether here it is malicious, though now it seems to lull the exhausted men to welcome sleep. The **half-rhymes** (or **pararhymes**) link their 'snow-dazed' 'faces' with their 'sun-dozed' dreams of home 'where the blackbird fusses' (21–4), the incomplete **rhymes** perhaps suggesting the unreality of their visions of peace. This time the final short line of the stanza has a more disturbing question, as though the unreality of their dreams could only be a precursor to death: 'Is it that we are dying?' (25). The next stanza continues the unreal dreams; their 'ghosts drag home' (26), but the archaic word 'glozed' warns us that this is all

CONTEXT

Owen described No Man's Land in a letter to his mother on 19 January 1917: 'It is like the eternal place of gnashing of teeth … It is pock-marked like a body of foulest disease and its odour is the breath of cancer. I have not seen any dead. I have done worse. In the dank air I have *perceived* it, and in the darkness, felt … No Man's Land under snow is like the face of the moon, chaotic, crater-ridden, uninhabitable, awful, the abode of madness.'

**CHECK
THE BOOK**

There is a detailed
exposition of
'Exposure' in
Chapter Nine of Jon
Silkin's *Out of Battle*
(Routledge, 1987).
Silkin points out
that in 1917, when
he wrote this poem,
Owen had just read
the English
translation of Henri
Barbusse's *Le Feu*
(*Under Fire*), a
graphic account of
life and death on
the Western Front
published in French
in 1916.

deceptive. The idyllic **pastoral** scene, in which fires are 'jewels' (27) and small creatures play, is 'closed' to them (29). (Jon Silkin points out that these lines recall in their delicate richness the work of John Keats, one of Owen's favourite poets – and Owen has already evoked Keats to **ironic** effect in the very first line of this poem, where 'Our brains ache' echoes 'my heart aches' from 'Ode to a Nightingale'.) Instead, they turn away from the harmless innocence of the vision to their task: 'dying' (30).

The seventh stanza is densely packed and capable of a number of readings – perhaps suggesting the conflicting thoughts in the minds of soldiers condemned to suffer in this 'eternal place of gnashing of teeth', as Owen described it. One interpretation is that their response to the reminder of home and country must be to fight in the defence of all they value most ('not otherwise can kind fires burn', 31). The ideas become still more complex in the next two lines. Owen could be suggesting that they fear that the destruction of the war will defeat even 'God's invincible spring' (33) – or that their very fighting over the right to possess nature is itself angering God. Their willing sacrifice ('not loath, we lie out here', 34) is undercut by the last phrase of the line: 'therefore were born'. Is this – this torment, this death – what they were born for? For the third time, the **refrain** ends with 'dying' (35) – this time, even 'love of God seems dying', implying either that the war has destroyed their faith in God or that God has withdrawn his love (Owen perhaps deliberately seeks to convey both meanings). This bitter conclusion seems reinforced in the final stanza by the punishment that nature (and therefore God, it seems) will bring with tonight's frost. The burying-party, in another pun, find that the 'eyes' of the dead 'are ice' (39). The refrain repeats for the final time that 'nothing happens', as if this inactivity is itself a punishment for those who 'only know war lasts' (12).

GLOSSARY		
26	glozed	deceived

WILFRED OWEN: INSENSIBILITY

- The poet says that men who have lost all feeling are happiest in wartime because they do not feel the loss of comrades or even their own sufferings.
- Those civilians who have no compassion are, however, wretched, utterly without feeling.

The poet describes a number of ways in which the feelings of soldiers are deadened by the war. They are 'happy' if they have no compassion for those who die, and do not feel their own suffering. If their imagination is deadened they will no longer be troubled by memories of bloodshed and they 'can laugh among the dying' (30). On leave, they can ignore those dying at the front. The uneducated soldier sings because of lack of feeling; those who think themselves wise might be better adopting his attitude. But the poet curses those civilians whose feelings have not been scarred in battle yet have no compassion for the suffering it causes.

COMMENTARY

Although the poem opens with the word 'Happy' and begins two further **stanzas** this way, Owen uses the word ironically. The title itself should warn the reader that this poem is about absence of feeling. This is evident in the number of negative terms that Owen employs: 'no', 'not', 'no one', 'nor' and 'never' maintain this emphasis throughout the poem. This tone is echoed in his use of words such as 'gaps' (9), 'losses' (10), 'unconcerned' (30) and those ending in 'less' ('relentless', 38, 'lashless', 43, and 'hapless', 56). 'Compassion' (3) is seen, in this despairing view, to be a mockery, when men have to walk on 'alleys cobbled with their brothers' (5), a disturbing image that recalls both the general fact that so many others have already died on the land they march over and the literal truth that bodies were so numerous that soldiers did indeed step on them (as Rosenberg's 'Dead Man's Dump', p. 185, reminds us). Owen says the front line 'withers' (6), then voices his contempt for the first time for those who would sentimentally seek to prettify this in empty **rhetoric**, for 'they are troops who fade' and 'poets'

CONTEXT

Owen is famous for coining the phrase 'the pity of war' – see 'Strange Meeting' (**Extended commentaries: Text 3**). A CD of classical music composed in 1914–18, popular songs of the war years, and readings from Owen's letters and poems called *The Pity of War* was released in 2005 (Orchid Classics).

---

tearful fooling' (7–8) should not disguise the reality that they are mere 'gaps for filling: / Losses' (9–10). The first **stanza** concludes with weary resignation in the triple-stressed phrase: 'no one bothers' (11), recalling the dull frustration of 'But nothing happens' in 'Exposure'.

The short second stanza moves from indifference to the fate of colleagues to lack of feeling even 'for themselves' (13). Here the stress in the line falls heavily on 'for', then fades, as the soldiers' own sense of self fades through necessary 'dullness' (14). Owen implies that when 'Chance', the likelihood of death, is more certain even than the week's pay, insensibility is best. 'Imagination' is another burden, the third stanza explains, when 'they have enough to carry with ammunition' (20). Better, Owen implies, not to think of the blood those bullets are intended to spill; he plays, in typical **half-rhyme**, on 'red' and 'rid' (23–4) to indicate the soldier's refusal to think of the significance of blood. This is developed in the **image** of the 'small-drawn' heart (27), which constricts blood and, by implication, heart-feelings of pity just as their senses have been dulled in the way a military surgeon might burn flesh to stop the loss of blood from a wound (28). The advantage – that they 'can laugh among the dying' (30) – is, in its cruelty, an indictment of the effect of war on human decency.

The fourth stanza introduces 'the lad whose mind was never trained' (34) – whose lack of education, Owen implies, is accompanied by an inability to feel too deeply. By contrast, 'we march taciturn' (37), aware of the approach of death which Owen conveys in two lines whose **rhythm** is 'relentless', culminating in the 'huger night' of death (38–9). Owen reveals in the fifth stanza that 'we' are the 'wise', by implication those who are 'trained' and who feel more deeply – who therefore should attempt to see the war through the 'blunt and lashless eyes' of the 'lad' (43). Owen's attitude, with its implication that those without education suffer less, could appear to be patronising. It seems that his purpose was to make the **ironic** point that learning and experience, which are so valued in civilian life, are a burden in wartime to those who, in his disturbing image, 'with a thought besmirch / Blood over all our soul' (40–1). Although this seems to apply to those who have

---

CONTEXT

Owen wrote to his mother in early October 1918: 'I came out in order to help these boys – directly by leading them as well as an officer can; indirectly, by watching their sufferings that I may speak of them as well as a pleader can.'

experienced battle, by using 'we' Owen invites us, as readers, to identify ourselves with this viewpoint. Owen is sympathetic towards the soldiers whose feelings have been stunned by battle; in the final stanza, by contrast, his mood turns to anger. The heavy emphasis of the opening line mimics the thump of artillery (50) – but civilians have no excuse, for they cannot claim the 'simplicity' (53) of lack of education nor the traumas of battle. In damning words, he says that 'By choice they made themselves immune / To pity' (54–5). The **half-rhymes** drive the reader forward through each pair of lines (and in the case of line 53, the internal rhyme speeds this) to the conclusion, where the short line is followed by a sudden slowing to finish on the emotive and high pitched word 'tears' (59). Despite what he claimed earlier about the advantages of insensibility, Owen makes a powerful call for both pity and anger 'when many leave these shores' (57). The images are apocalyptic: 'shores' (57) has echoes of classical mythology's Lethe, the river of forgetfulness that the dead cross as they enter Hades (Hell); and 'the last sea and the hapless stars' (56) suggest the end of the world overlooked by an indifferent universe. It is, however, possible to detect a shift from the bleak conclusion of 'Exposure', since here Owen implies that it is worth directing curses at the brutality of those who want to continue war in the hope that they will see and feel 'pity and whatever moans in man' (55) before the end of the world descends.

 CHECK THE POEM
Owen refers to the 'kind old sun' in 'Futility' (p. 193), where, as in the sixth stanza here, it seems to be taunting humanity. He concludes: 'what made fatuous sunbeams toil / To break earth's sleep at all?'

GLOSSARY	
3	fleers mocks, laughs at
17	shilling a reference to the soldiers' pay and also perhaps to 'taking the King's shilling', a term used to describe enlisting in the armed forces
18	decimation destruction of a large proportion
28	cautery the process of destroying living tissue by applying a hot instrument (here applied to cauterising feelings)
29	ironed the heated metal used to cauterise the men's senses
40	besmirch stain

ROBERT GRAVES: RECALLING WAR

- Time has healed the wounds of war; the poem looks back twenty years to a time of rage, death and primitive ways of living that overpowered the forces of civilisation.
- Looking back, the war seems childish, as we anticipate even greater conflicts.

The wounded (of the First World War) have become so adjusted to their injuries that, twenty years later, they take them for granted. Yet at the time the war seemed like a disease that infected everyone with a kind of rage and claimed the lives of the young. Graves argues the fragility of human life changes our perspectives: basic needs become more important than art or learning. Looking back, the war feels like a game with toys – whilst we earnestly consider a future in which war could be even more destructive.

CHECK THE POEM

Another poem looking back, but not nearly so far, is Edward Thomas's 'In Memoriam (Easter 1915)'. Thomas died in 1917.

COMMENTARY

Graves wrote this poem in 1938, as the reference to 'twenty years ago' (7) implies. By that time Europe was once again bracing itself for war (civil war had already broken out in Spain in 1936), so Graves's picture at the end of the poem of 'yet more boastful visions of despair' would have been a painfully topical reference when the poem was first read, with news of German planes bombing the Spanish city of Guernica fresh in the memory. The opening **stanza**, however, calmly describes a series of injuries from bullet wound, through loss of limbs to blindness, that men have adjusted to as if they were natural. Graves's **image** in the first line of the wound 'silvered clean' sets the tone of clinical distance that is echoed in the relaxed **rhythm** of his **blank verse**. Yet the **simile** at the end of the stanza is a reminder that the effects of that 'wild night-stumbling' (10) are permanent, as the repetition of the pattern of 'The one-legged man ... / The one-armed man' in lines 3 and 4 emphasises.

Graves moves in the second stanza to his central question: 'What, then, was war?' (11). It is as though he fears that, as soldiers forget their wounds, society will fail to recall what persuaded men that

they had 'the duty to run mad' (37). He spends the next three
stanzas answering this. His language becomes darker: war was 'an
infection' (12) that produced 'Boastful tongue, clenched fist and
valiant yard' (16). 'Valiant' and the reference to swords, a weapon of
older wars, introduces an **ironic** tone that Graves develops at the
end of the stanza, where his **oxymoronic** picture of 'Death' as
'patron alone / Of healthy dying' (18–19) is a reminder of how
many young lives were lost. The next stanza describes other
changes, the **alliteration** of the opening line placing an ironic
emphasis on 'fine' followed by the contradictions of 'sick with
delight'. These 'fine bed-fellows' were a concentration on 'all-flesh'
at the expense of thought (22), with perhaps also an echo of the
New Testament words on human frailty: 'all flesh is as grass, and all
the glory of man as the flower of grass' (1 Peter 1:24). Graves raises
the ironic **rhetoric** in the remaining lines in the third stanza, in
which the 'antiqueness of romance' (23) and 'tasty honey oozing
from the heart' (24) remind readers of the sentimental language of
the patriotic poets and press that Graves mocked in his memoir
Goodbye to All That in 1929. 'Wine, meat, log-fires, a roof over the
head' (26) continues the cosy theme of old adventure stories – only
to demolish it in the last three lines, in which God is used only as an
oath because, of course, there were no such comforts, only 'wounds
beyond all surgeoning' (30). He drops the **satire** for a more direct
attack on war in the fourth stanza, where war is seen as 'extinction'
(33) of all that enabled humanity to rise above mere brutality ('art
and faith ... logic ... love', 33–5). War's 'unendurable moment' (36)
inverts all that is sane by imposing 'the duty to run mad' (37) – a
powerful reminder of the blood-lust that warfare needed to instil in
soldiers about to launch an attack.

The final stanza brings the poem back to the present, again looking
with apparent detachment on the war. Graves resorts to a jocular
tone: 'the merry ways of guns' (38) are twice described as 'like a
child' (40–1) and the references continue with 'toy-like' and 'tin-
soldiers' (42–3). The childishness of this attitude is contrasted to the
'elder days' of wisdom and adulthood (44). Graves's irony has the
last word, however; in the last line the emphasis falls on the words
'boastful' and 'despair'. These 'visions' are not of improvement, but
of the failure of humanity to learn the lessons of the last war.

> **CONTEXT**
>
> Graves himself was
> seriously wounded
> during the Battle
> of the Somme in
> 1916; his parents
> were told he had
> died and he had
> the pleasure of
> asking *The Times*,
> which had listed
> him as killed, to
> print: 'Captain
> Robert Graves,
> Royal Welch
> Fusiliers, officially
> reported died of
> wounds, wishes to
> inform his friends
> that he is
> recovering from
> his wounds at
> Queen Alexandra's
> Hospital'
> (*Goodbye to All
> That*, p. 189).

GLOSSARY

1	**silvered** the skin is made smooth by the scars, like silver
16	**yard** short for 'yard of steel', that is the blade of a sword (taken as a yard, or just under a metre, in length)
32	**foundering of sublimities** wrecking of belief in higher feelings

CONTEXT

The Battle of Marathon in 490 BC was a decisive victory by the Greeks over a larger Persian force in which the Persians sustained heavy losses. According to legend, an Athenian messenger ran 40 km to Athens with news of the victory before dying of exhaustion – a tale that became the basis of the modern marathon race.

CONTEXT

The main account of the battle comes from the Greek historian Herodotus, who, however, was not born until a few years after the battle. Graves could have had in mind the disastrous allied attempt to seize the Gallipoli peninsula from Turkey in 1915.

ROBERT GRAVES: THE PERSIAN VERSION

- Persians adopt a different view to the Greeks of the Battle of Marathon; it was only a skirmish in which the Persian forces fought valiantly.

The poem gives 'the Persian version' of the Battle of Marathon which is better known from the Greek perspective. Persians see it as a 'trivial skirmish' (2) rather than an attempt to invade Greece. In the circumstances the Persians acquitted themselves well.

COMMENTARY

This poem dates from the 1940s and, as in 'Recalling War', Graves adopts a detached, cool tone. There is no reference to twentieth-century events, though readers of Graves's memoir *Goodbye to All That* will not be surprised at his contempt for 'official versions' of events that he (and readers of the newspapers) would have been familiar with in the First World War. The title indicates the tone that Graves has the **persona** of his poem adopt: an apparently plausible attempt to put the record straight. The fact that the two words of the title **rhyme** makes the words sound glib, insincere – and the opening 'Truth-loving' confirms this. Apart from suggesting that there may be other Persians who are *not* 'truth-loving', the term implies that the speaker will rely on asserting a version of the story as truth (and depicting the Greeks as liars) rather than proving it. This manipulation of language continues by describing the battle which involved perhaps 25,000 men as a 'trivial skirmish' (2) and attempts to diminish it further by disputing even the location: it was merely 'near Marathon' (2). The Greek accounts are characterised as a 'theatrical tradition' (3), as though the Greeks, famed for their drama, were merely making up another play, and the speaker continues to diminish the scale of the battle by words such as 'mere reconnaissance' (5) made with 'obsolete / Light craft' (7–8). The claims rise to a peak of absurdity as the rout of the Persian forces (a Greek scholar, Graves would expect his readers to know that Herodotus records that 6,400 Persians and only 192 Athenians perished) is described as 'salutary' (14) and carried out 'magnificently' (16). The regular **rhythm** places the emphasis on the neat rhymes, which themselves suggest an account that is too neat, too rehearsed. This is disrupted somewhat at line 10, where the line pattern is broken by the **caesura** after 'Greece', as though the speaker's voice rises in anger at such a suggestion, only to fall onto the word 'contempt' at the end of the line. This is followed by a shorter line as the speaker attempts the audacious feat of turning the defeat into victory – the uneven **metre** here conveying the verbal trickery in which the word 'only' hides the claim to reverse the facts of history.

QUESTION

What does this poem have to say about history and how it is made?

EDMUND BLUNDEN: THE ZONNEBEKE ROAD

QUESTION

Like Blunden in line 29, Owen describes the barbed wire as 'brambles' in 'Exposure' (p. 189), another poem describing the front line in the depths of winter. What differences do you notice between the ways the two poets respond to this situation?

- Day breaks over a trench in the grip of winter. A group of soldiers suffer in the bitter cold but defy death.

As dawn comes a group of men stand down after their first night on duty. The place is desolate and depresses the poet. Apart from the German mortars, the men are threatened by the bitter cold; their only answer is to treat the threat of death with disdain.

COMMENTARY

The poem is a graphic description of the bitter cold of an early winter morning in the trenches as the men complete the first night of a week's tour of duty. The scene is bleak and danger threatens everywhere. Blunden, whose love of nature led him to describe himself in his memoir, *Undertones of War*, as 'a harmless young shepherd in a soldier's coat', reflects bitterly that dawn no longer has the same 'merry flame / Which the young day was wont to fling through space!' (2–3). The very energy of the verb 'fling' seems completely out of place in this lifeless location, where instead of delight at a new day, 'Agony stares from each grey face' (4). The light is 'late' and 'withered' (1), matching the men's faces. The **narrator**, who draws the reader in by speaking as if to a fellow-soldier, points out 'that iron man' shaving, in a short line that contrasts with the one that follows it: 'Go ask him, shall we win?' (10). The narrator implies that the answer is so obvious the question is ridiculous. (Blunden wrote about the first day of the Battle of the Somme, 1 July 1916: 'By the end of the day both sides had seen, in the sad scrawl of broken earth and murdered men, the answer to the question. No road. No thoroughfare. Neither race had won, nor could win, the War. The War had won, and would go on winning' *The Mind's Eye*, 1934.)

Blunden **personifies** the hostility of the environment. Here, there is no 'young day', only the broken dugout looking, in a grim **metaphor**, as if a rotting 'corpse' is under the ground (14), which he characterises as 'seeming-saturnine / For no good cause' (16–17). In fact, the enemy shelling is cause enough to fear the place, as line 20 explains. The stones are imagined to 'flinch' in the bitter wind (22) and Blunden makes the sky into a suffering face, with 'its clay cheek' (both colourless and heavy) impaled on trees that, 'shell-chopped', have become fangs (26). The hostile personification continues as 'the ice-bound throat gulps out a gargoyle shriek' (27), where the awkwardness of the **assonance** conveys the harsh weather. Even the light is unpleasant, described as if it were muddy water, the **alliteration** emphasising the drabness: 'the daylight oozes into dun' (30). If earlier the idea of 'winning' had seemed folly, the final four lines provide an alternative, desperate kind of hope: the narrator addresses 'dull clashing death' (34) and, against the power that 'shreds ... grass ... homes and men' (35) throws back their own icy 'disdain' (37). These four lines, in contrast to the regular **rhyme** of the rest of the poem, are only **half-rhymes** – as if to suggest the uncertain nature of 'that one hope' (37).

GLOSSARY

14	chaps cheeks
16	saturnine gloomy
18	Haymarket a communication trench, named after a busy street in central London
20	minenwerfers German mortar (literally 'mine-thrower'), whose bombs would fall straight down on the trench
29	bine twining stem of a plant such as bindweed

CHECK THE POEM

Other poems which refer to dawn include Hardy's 'Men Who March Away' (p. 160), McCrae's 'In Flanders Fields' (p. 165), Rosenberg's 'Break of Day in the Trenches' (p. 184), Owen's 'Futility' (p. 193), Bishop's 'In the Dordogne' (p. 203), Binyon's 'For the Fallen' (p. 209) and Cannan's 'Rouen' (p. 220). Compare the different treatments of the dawn.

EDMUND BLUNDEN: VLAMERTINGHE: PASSING THE CHÂTEAU, JULY 1917

- Soldiers advancing to the front pass a garden overflowing with flowers. It is of little comfort to those thinking more about the blood that will be shed in the battle ahead.

The abundant flowers the soldiers see on the way to battle seem to be a reminder of impending death. The rich colours, however, are not quite the same as the red blood that will soon be shed.

COMMENTARY

This poem, with its opening quotation from a famous poem by Keats, is both a tribute to the beauties of nature and an **ironic** comment on the destructions of war. The stately beauty of Keats's line, describing an imagined scene from classical antiquity, is immediately contrasted with the emphasis that this is no mythical scene: 'But we are coming to the sacrifice' (2), where the stress falls pointedly on 'we'. The **narrator** moves between innocent admiration of the flowers to this personal identification with the soldiers, voiced most forcefully in the unexpected **colloquial** 'mate' in line 13. This uneasy combination is evident in the third and fourth lines, where the repeated formula ('Must those have flowers who ...? / May those have flowers who ...?') voices the contrast between 'flowers' and 'gone West' (their doom) and 'death and lice' (the sordid realities of their lives). The contrasts are pointed up in

CONTEXT

'The road towards Vlamertinghe ... took one presently through a gorgeous and careless multitude of poppies and sorrels and bull-daisies to the ground of Vlamertinghe Château, many windowed, not much hurt, but looking very dismal in the pitiless perfect sun' (Blunden, *Undertones of War*, 1928, ch. 20).

Poetry of the First World War **63**

CHECK THE POEM

The opening line is a quotation from 'Ode on a Grecian Urn' by John Keats (1795–1821). It describes scenes that decorate the urn; just before the line quoted by Blunden, Keats writes: 'Who are these coming to the sacrifice?'

CHECK THE NET

Edmund Blunden is one of the poets you can hear on the Poetry Archive at **www. poetryarchive. org.** He comments on and reads two of his war poems, including 'Report on Experience' (p. 199).

the next four lines, where the 'proud mansion borrows grace for grace' (7), such is the beauty of the flowers that surround the château – but we are reminded of the presence of war with an echo of Keats, who had described the 'heifer lowing at the skies' – where Blunden has ' brute guns lowing' (8). The poem concludes with further celebration of the flowers, though the reader is probably by now thinking of an **ironic** association of 'bubbling roses' and bubbling blood and of the 'poppies' that flowered over the battlefields (10–11). The **pastoral** image is shattered completely by the grim comment of the final two lines; 'this red should have been much duller' (14) because it did not match the actual colour of blood – and because the reality is much 'duller' than the bright hopes such beauty in times gone would have evoked in poets. The form seems to indicate this use of convention yet subverts it; the poem has fourteen lines, so is to all intents and purposes a **sonnet**, yet both the **rhyme** and **metre** are irregular. Blunden ends, as might be expected, with a forceful rhyme to convey his message ('colour/duller') yet the last line is far longer than expected, and breaks out of formality into everyday speech.

GLOSSARY		
3	gone West **colloquial** expression meaning 'died'
12	damask a damask rose is red or pink
12	vermilion bright scarlet

EDGELL RICKWORD: WINTER WARFARE

- The poet imagines cold as an officer visiting the battlefield to inflict torment on the troops.

The poem **personifies** the bitter winter as 'Colonel Cold', freezing everything at the front. The weather was the same for the enemy; as in No Man's Land the cold attacks the wounded from both sides.

COMMENTARY

This short poem uses a deceptively jaunty **ballad rhythm** to describe the torments inflicted on the troops by the bitter winter at the front. Unlike Owen in 'Exposure' and Blunden in 'The Zonnebeke Road' (pp. 189 and 198), Rickword offers no indication of the soldiers' reactions, though his introduction of a German version of 'Colonel Cold' in line 15 implies the indiscriminate nature of the suffering at the front. The personification of the cold as a military officer is precise and sustained, from his 'tabs … and spurs' (2) and his inspection of the front line to finally moving across No Man's Land where he kills off the wounded. No one escapes, not even the 'lice' (4). Like Blunden's men, the soldiers here have 'fingers stuck to biting steel' (7). The third **stanza** seems more picturesque, with the barbed wire given 'fleecy wool' by the frost (10) and iron 'snapping' like 'sugar sticks' (11–12). This deceptive picture is countered by the final stanza, in which the cold brutally stabs those who have already been 'torn by screaming steel' (20). The language echoes the effects of the cold, in which everything is stiffened and the frost intensifies sounds, as 'tinkling spurs' (17) suggests.

QUESTION

Another war poem which uses the ballad form is Gurney's 'Ballad of the Three Spectres' (p. 181). Compare these two poems. What similarities and differences in both subject matter and style seem interesting to you?

GLOSSARY

2	**tabs** badges on the collar of an officer
2	**rime** thick white frost
15	**Hauptmann Kälte** Captain Cold (German)

E. E. CUMMINGS: 'NEXT TO OF COURSE GOD AMERICA I'

- The poem parodies a patriotic speech praising the glorious dead who gave themselves for liberty.

The poem is in the form of a fragment of a speech by a patriotic **orator** in praise of America and her heroic war dead. He breaks off at the end to drink a glass of water.

Commentary

The unconventional typography and punctuation of Cummings's work comes as a shock after the largely conventional verse that precedes it in *The Oxford Book of War Poetry*. Cummings, who published this poem in 1926, was heavily influenced by the **modernist** poets such as Pound and Eliot, whose work features a little later in the anthology. Unlike Eliot (for example in 'Triumphal March', p. 211), whose references range across Western culture, Cummings uses fragments from nationalist songs and the empty **rhetoric** of public oratory to **satirise** the patriotic rhetoric that, he implies, deceived the public during wartime.

CHECK THE BOOK

Ben Elton's 2005 historical novel, *The First Casualty*, follows Douglas Kingsley, a detective and conscientious objector, who is released from prison in 1917 to investigate the murder of a British soldier convalescing behind his own lines.

Despite its disregard of the rules, the poem does in fact conform to the requirements of a **sonnet**; Cummings even breaks the word 'beaut-/iful' over lines 9 and 10 in order to provide a **rhyme** for the final word, 'mute'. One effect of the absence of most capital letters and punctuation is to give a sense of breathless rush, as though the speaker were swept away by his own **clichés**. The **register** is a mix of the grandiose, with its quotations from 'The Star Spangled Banner' and 'My country, 'tis of thee' (lines 2–4), and **colloquial**, with 'next to of course god america i / love you' (1–2) and 'by jingo by gee by gosh by gum' (8). The rhetoric is in places meaningless ('centuries come and go / and are no more what of it we should worry', 4–5) or simply reveals the pointlessness of death in battle: 'they did not stop to think they died instead' (12). The speech rises to a climax with a question ('shall the voice of liberty be mute?', 13) which has no connection with what has been said so far. The **parody** is completed by the **bathos** of the final line, in which the tone changes from the pompous invocation of 'the voice of liberty' to 'And drank rapidly a glass of water'. The awkward position of 'rapidly' exaggerates the descent to the mundaneness of the situation, as does the separation of this line from the rest of the sonnet.

Cummings's attitude towards public rhetoric, also seen in 'my sweet old etcetera' (p. 201), was at least in part the result of his own experiences in wartime, when he served for a while as an ambulance driver before being imprisoned on false charges by the French. He became a pacifist, an attitude reflected in the poem 'i sing of Olaf glad and big' (p. 202), about 'a conscientious object-or'.

JOHN PEALE BISHOP: IN THE DORDOGNE

- Soldiers staying in a French castle surrounded by the beauties of nature and reminders of the age of chivalry go out to die in modern battles.

The poem opens in the early morning in a French castle; soldiers shave, then pass a religious statue and see trees as they go on duty. The many dead are brought back to be buried under the shadow of a tower that dates from the time of **chivalry** and **romance** (when heroes in the Middle Ages set out on adventures). The beauty of the setting contrasts with the deaths of the men.

COMMENTARY

The short, three-line, first **stanza** sounds as though this will be another description of trench life. The **alliteration** in lines 2 and 3 is a device seen in Owen and others. In the second stanza, however, the poem describes a more picturesque setting which sounds, with its 'stone stairs', 'spur chains' and 'cocks' (4–7) as though it were from an historical romance – there are even 'ghosts of a dead dawn' (8), whose presence remains 'crouched on the staircase' (10) to lend a slightly sinister atmosphere to the scene. Bishop sustains this uncertainty in the next stanza, though the hints of death increase. The 'Virgin and Child', who could be offering the soldiers protection, are 'serene' (15) but, following the slight pause of the line break, he adds, 'Who were stone' (16). The 'sycamores' recall 'three aged mages' (17) – the Wise Men bringing gifts to the Christ-child – but their 'gifts of gold' (18), dying leaves and the 'autumn odors' (19) are reminders of decay and death that are picked up in the final stanza, where Bishop explicitly links the two: 'the leaves fell / And were blown away; the young men rotted / Under the shadow of the tower' (41–3).

CHECK THE POEM
Another American poet who made a link between death and autumn is Wallace Stevens in 'The Death of a Soldier' (p. 169).

The fourth stanza makes clear that the men leave this beautiful setting only to be killed by 'thousands' (23), 'gassed' (25) in modern, industrialised warfare and buried under 'the tower of the troubadours' (28). The contrast between the ideals, **symbolised** by

QUESTION

Compare John Peale Bishop's use of **motifs** from the age of **chivalry** with Herbert Asquith's in 'The Volunteer' (p. 163). What differences do you notice in the effects of these references in the two poems?

romantic castles and love poetry, and the grim reality is explored in the fifth stanza. 'We thought something must come of it', Bishop has the soldiers say (33), only to make clear that indifference is the response. The statue of the Virgin and the trees are alike unmoved and 'The colonel slept on' (40). Unlike some other war poets, Bishop ends not in anger but by emphasising the beauty of the scene; the romantic associations of 'ravelling curtains' (41) and the 'blue and azure veils' of the evening (46) – which the idealistic youths no longer see as they rot underground.

GLOSSARY

12	**bed of Sully** 'Sully' could refer to the twelfth-century Bishop Maurice de Sully, who oversaw the building of the Cathedral of Notre-Dame de Paris, or the statesman Maximilien de Béthune, Duc de Sully (1560–1641); the point Bishop seems to be making is that the colonel is sleeping in comfort, perhaps dreaming of the romantic past, whilst his men go off to fight and die
17	**mages** magicians or magi, the reference is to the Wise Men who brought gifts to the infant Jesus (see lines 15 and 18)
27	**Périgord** area in France famous for its medieval and Renaissance castles along the Dordogne and Vézère rivers; the area was at times under English control until the fifteenth century, hence the reference to 'the English tower' (39)
28	**troubadours** medieval French poets who wrote about an idealised form of love

DAVID JONES: *FROM* IN PARENTHESIS

- A company of soldiers advances on the enemy lines; death claims many, including the officer in charge.

The extract describes an attack on a wood held by the Germans; as the men advance in line many are killed. They run for the trees under shell-fire whilst the Sergeant tries to keep order. Mr Jenkins, their officer, is hit and falls.

COMMENTARY

This extract from *In Parenthesis* can appear daunting at first glance, as Jones mixes an account of an attack during the Battle of the Somme with elements from Arthurian legend, Welsh myths and the Bible in a loose **free-verse** style. It is more approachable if read first as an **impressionistic** account of the confusion of battle before turning attention to the wider context Jones invokes by reference to history, religion and myth. Jones himself was a member of the 15th (London Welsh) Service Battalion of the Royal Welch Fusiliers which consisted, as its name implies, of a mix of volunteers from London and Wales. The central character in the **narrative** is Private Ball, who is mentioned towards the end of this extract and who is one of the few to survive. The extract in *The Oxford Book of War Poetry* is taken from Part 7 of the work. Part 1 describes parade and embarkation for France; Part 2 is about training in France and the march towards the front; in Part 3 the men continue their march and relieve another regiment holding the trenches; Part 4 is a detailed description of trench life; Part 5 continues their time in the trenches, followed by a period of rest and the march towards the Somme; in Part 6 they rest before the battle and move into position for the attack on the German defences in Mametz Wood on 10 July 1916 which features in Part 7.

The extract opens with an indirect reference to the slaughter that had already begun. As in classical poetry, death is **personified** as claiming soldiers individually though Jones makes this a disturbing **image** of an incestuous 'sweet sister death' (1) who in her debauchery claims men as her lovers. The bodies then are left to 'nourish a lesser category of being' (9) – just as the worms have eaten the dead of the past conflicts. By naming these ancient heroes, Jones is ennobling his humble soldiers. The rest of the extract is concerned with the chaos and destruction of the present, in which the soldiers' heightened senses record a confusing kaleidoscope of impressions. Even here, however, Jones points up references to the apocalyptic curse of war in the last book of the Bible ('red horses', 36) and the trial of faith recorded in the Book of Daniel (the 'counter-barrage warms to the seventh power', 43). The tumbling lines, sometimes reading like prose but yet with the careful artistry

> **CONTEXT**
>
> Like Isaac Rosenberg, David Jones was an artist before he took up writing and he, too, served as a private soldier during the war. He began *In Parenthesis* in 1928 but it was not completed and published, with the support of T. S. Eliot, until 1937.

of poetry, convey the pandemonium ('burn boat and sever every tie every held thing goes west and / tethering snapt', 37–8). Alongside the horror and disruption to the senses caused by the bombardment ('The immediate foreground sheers up', 40), Jones introduces the familiar shapes of his humble companions: 'Lazarus Cohen ... his entrenching-tool-blade-carrier hung low (50–1). As the men approach the wood Jones draws attention with precision to the natural features: 'at the margin / straggle tangled oak and flayed sheeny beech-bole and fragile / birch', where the 'fresh stalks bled' as if in sympathy with the men (85–9). In the same place, however, there is the cruel hardware of war: 'cork-screw stapled trip wire' (91). The description of the death of Mr Jenkins at the end of the extract is as if in slow motion. Jones lends the officer's final moments a mixture of heroic and religious dignity, as he 'sinks on one knee / and now on the other' (103–4) as if in prayer, then, neatly linking the man's swaying 'lanyard' to a pendulum, describes his ebbing life as 'the clock run down' (107–9). The 'iron saucer' of his helmet (110) slips over his face so that both literally and **metaphorically** he is 'blind against the morning' (117) as he falls at the altar where his life has been sacrificed (118–20).

In Parenthesis is sometimes described as an **epic** – a long **narrative** poem recounting heroic acts in the history of a nation – but this term does not adequately describe Jones's work. Unlike the classical epic, his central characters are humble infantrymen and their story does not have any overarching narrative, nor does it lead to some heroic achievement. This is in part because of the huge scale and fragmented nature of modern conflict; there might be individual acts of heroism but they have little effect on the outcome of battle. Despite this, Jones is at pains to place his modern soldiers alongside warriors of the past, as the opening section of this extract shows with its list of names from Arthurian and Welsh legends and references to the Battle of Thermopylae and the Bible. He concludes by giving religious significance to the death of Mr Jenkins. Jones is the only **modernist** poet in *The Oxford Book of War Poetry* who had first-hand experience of combat; he was encouraged to publish his work by T. S. Eliot, whose work it in some ways resembles. In particular, Jones uses a mix of **free verse** and prose, a fragmentary approach to construction (though always with an overarching

CHECK THE POEM

In Parenthesis is not an easy book to find and is often out of print. There is a longer extract from Part 7, beginning at the same point as in *The Oxford Book of War Poetry* and continuing to the end of the work, in Jon Silkin's *Penguin Book of First World War Poetry* (1979).

structure in mind) and places learned references alongside **colloquial** speech, archaic spellings and the vocabulary of modern warfare. The very title, meaning 'between brackets' suggests a digression; Jones wrote in the preface to the work that the war years took place 'in a kind of space between – I don't know between quite what – but as you turn aside to do something'. The work has, however, a consistent vision and his references are all designed to lend events a mythic dimension. The final lines of *In Parenthesis* are a reminder of its basis in his own experience and his intention to convey the importance of what 'all common and hidden men and ... secret princes' went through: 'the man who does not know this has not understood anything'.

CHECK THE NET

There is a useful account of *In Parenthesis*, with illustrations from Jones's own drawings at **www.case.edu**. Find the College of Arts and Sciences homepage and search for 'Landscapes of David Jones'.

GLOSSARY

11–14	**Tristram ... Alisand le Orphelin [Alisander le Orphelin in Malory] Beaumains** Knights of the Round Table in Malory's *Morte d'Arthur*
16	**Thermopylae** battle in 480 BC in which an outnumbered Greek force held off a large Persian army
17	**Balin and Balan** brothers in Malory's *Morte d'Arthur* who kill each other in combat
20	**Gelboe** the mountain where King Saul and his sons, including David's close friend Jonathan (line 19), were killed by the Philistines (Old Testament, I Samuel 31; it is called Gilboa in the King James Version but Jones uses the form found in Roman Catholic translations)
21	**Absalom** son of King David who rebelled against his father and was killed (Old Testament, II Samuel 18)
36	**red horses** in the New Testament Book of Revelation (or the Apocalypse), the red horse is generally taken to symbolise war: 'and power was given to him that sat thereon to take peace from the earth and that they should kill one another' (Revelation 6:4)
43	**seventh power** Jones's note refers to 'Daniel, ch iii': this is the Old Testament story of Shadrach, Meshach and Abednego who were thrown into a 'burning fiery furnace' heated 'seven times more than it was wont to be heated'. In the furnace, they were seen to be talking to a fourth man – whom Jones calls 'the Second Person of the Blessed Trinity', that is Jesus Christ

continued

CONTEXT

See also David
Jones's own notes
at the end of the
extract from *In
Parenthesis* in *The
Oxford Book of
War Poetry*, p. 208.

58	**'02 Weavel** Private Weavel ('02 are the last two digits of his army number, which in full would be something like 01502)
70	**albescent** shading into white
107	**lanyard** a cord hung round the neck, often with a whistle attached
112	**ventaille** in medieval armour, a covering for the lower part of the face
118	**predella** platform on which an altar stands in a church

LAURENCE BINYON: FOR THE FALLEN

- An elegy to those who have died in defence of England, who will never be forgotten.

England's dead are celebrated with solemn ceremony; they will be remembered for ever for their bravery in defence of freedom.

COMMENTARY

Binyon's solemn **elegy**, with its praise for the heroic young, 'straight of limb, true of eye, steady and aglow' (10), seems rather out of place at this point in Stallworthy's selection, following the brutal **realism**, **satire** or even despair of poets of the later years of the war. It presumably comes here because, although written at the very outbreak of the war, it is a poem most associated with the remembrance ceremonies that were instituted after the Armistice, and Stallworthy therefore places it alongside poems looking back on the conflict.

The poem has a stately gravity resulting from its measured pace and carefully placed pauses. The first and third lines of each **stanza** are longer and in most cases broken by a **caesura** denoted by a punctuation mark, as in the first line. This pattern is echoed, though not quite so strongly, in the third line, which is of a similar length. The second and fourth lines are shorter and they **rhyme** – the last line of each stanza is the shortest. The effect of this can be heard by reading the famous fourth stanza; it is not surprising that this has become a feature of public remembrance ceremonies. Binyon uses a repetitive pattern found in Hebrew poetry known as parallelism that would have been familiar to his readers through the Psalms of the Old Testament. 'They shall grow not old' is followed by the almost identical 'as we that are left grow old' (13) and the next line has a similar balance, ending with 'condemn' (to have echoed exactly with 'condemn them' would have not only made the line too long but also concluded on a weak stress). The third line is again carefully balanced not only in sound but also by evoking both the beginning and end of the day, with their associations of birth and death. The final line of the stanza is less than half the length of the first line; the effect is to slow the reader down to a funeral pace, in which each syllable is stressed and lengthened as if to match the earlier lines in duration.

The confident faith in the justice of 'England's' cause, 'the cause of the free' (4), is a sign that this was written at the outbreak of war and is doubtless another reason it seemed appropriate for official ceremonies. The vocabulary is marked by high **rhetoric**: 'Solemn the drums thrill: Death August and royal' (5) is followed by reference to 'immortal spheres' and 'glory' (6, 8). The poem ends by placing the dead among 'the stars ... / Moving in marches upon the heavenly plain' (25–6). Binyon's rhetoric is not the enthusiastic welcoming of war that sounds in some of Brooke's **sonnets**; he acknowledges 'the time of our darkness' (27) but attributes a solemn dignity to the sacrifices that are being made.

> **CONTEXT**
>
> Binyon's poem was first published in *The Times* on 21 September 1914. Binyon was too old to serve in the forces but spent much of his annual leave during the war working as a volunteer Red Cross medical orderly in France. The fourth stanza is regularly recited at Remembrance Day services in November throughout the United Kingdom each year.

EZRA POUND: *FROM* HUGH SELWYN MAUBERLEY

- A survey of the reasons men fought, what they learnt and what they found on their return from the War.

The poem lists a range of reasons why men fought in the War and their disillusionment on their return home to discover lies and corruption were flourishing. They had shown heroism and seen horrors and many 'of the best' (29) had died – all for a worthless, rotten culture.

COMMENTARY

Pound described *Hugh Selwyn Mauberley* as 'a farewell to London' and it is at least in part autobiographical, describing his development as a poet (Hugh Selwyn Mauberley is an imaginary minor English poet of the 1890s who has some similarities with Pound). The work consists of eighteen short poems, grouped into two sections. *The Oxford Book of War Poetry* prints the final two poems, IV and V (the latter begins, after the asterisk, at the top of page 211, with 'There died a myriad', 28) of the first section in which Pound voices a reaction to the state of the nation after the War. The extract here looks disjointed and disorganised but this is deceptive; probably the best way to approach the poem is to read it aloud and hear the ways Pound creates climaxes and **rhetorical** effects.

The 'in any case' of the opening line gives the impression of casualness, though its repetition in line 3 should alert the reader to Pound's craft, in which fragmentation and compression play an important part. The second 'in any case' is an indication that, as only 'some' believed that they were fighting 'pro domo' (3), other motives were also present. Pound elaborates this in the second **stanza**, where the **anaphora** ('some for ... some from ...', 5–8) neatly points up the contradictions in motives for fighting, from 'adventure' to 'love of slaughter' – and how the experience of battle overturned these. The reversal does not even need spelling out – the ellipsis after 'learning later' (9) makes the reader's completion ('learning later to hate slaughter') more effective for being unspoken, but made obvious by the opposite situation he describes for the fearful: 'learning love of slaughter' (10). The stanza pivots around the fragments from the Latin tag that Owen had also dismissed with contempt (by writing this as 'non "dulce" non "et decor"', 12: Pound indicates that the tag is broken now, defective). The transformation that Pound believed had occurred is powerfully summarised in a single line: 'believing in old men's lies, then unbelieving' (14). This captures the frustration that writers such as Owen, Sassoon and others felt when returning home on leave to

CONTEXT

Pound was an American who (like his close friend T. S. Eliot) lived in Britain during the First World War. He was in influential figure in the **Imagist** and **Modernist** movements. *Hugh Selwyn Mauberley* was published in 1920, the year he left London for Paris. Two years later Eliot wrote in his long poem *The Waste Land*, in an echo of the final part of this extract as well as of Dante's *Inferno*: 'I had not thought death had undone so many.'

read and hear patriotic sentiments and propaganda that bore no relation to the 'hell' (13) they had experienced. Again Pound uses anaphora ('home to ...', 16–17) to emphasise what the troops found on their return, and does not flinch from blunt condemnation of profiteering and 'liars' (19). Pound summarises in similarly terse manner the 'wastage' (20) of the war – and having used that word, he needs only to mention 'fine bodies' (22) to make clear what became of them. **Alliteration** ('fair ..., fine ... / fortitude ... / frankness', 22–4) links the bodies and bravery to the responses. Again these are compressed, with 'disillusions' (25) emphasised by its place at the beginning of the line, to be followed by the macabre 'laughter out of dead bellies' (27).

The eight-line poem that forms the conclusion of this extract is an even more concentrated version of Pound's indictment of society as he saw it. '[A] myriad' (28) died – and for what? 'For an old bitch gone in the teeth' (30). Pound's words convey forcefully his contempt for what 'civilization' (31) has become: just 'broken statues' and 'battered books' (34–5). It is an **image** that recalls the actual destruction of the war (the sacking of the ancient library at Louvain by the German army, for instance) and the way that the old values and certainties of the pre-war world had been swept away to be replaced, in Pound's eyes, by shabby commercialism and superficiality.

Pound's indictment of 'old men's lies' expresses a view widely held by those who had experienced the war at first hand, expressed with less venom by Blunden in 'Report on Experience' ('This is not what we were formerly told', p. 199) and heard in Cummings's words: 'my father used / to become hoarse talking about how it was / a privilege and if only he / could' ('my sweet old etcetera', p. 201).

Owen's poem 'Parable of the Old Men and the Young' also ends by blaming the 'old man' for slaying 'half the seed of Europe, one by one'. Along with the image of ruins (seen in T. S. Eliot's choice of title for his long poem of 1922, *The Waste Land*), the gulf between the Old Men and the Young was to become part of the enduring myth of the war.

 **QUESTION**

All soldiers who entered a theatre of war were presented with the Victory Medal that bore the inscription 'The Great War for Civilisation'. What is Pound's opinion of the 'civilisation' these men came home to?

 CHECK THE NET

Pound can be heard reading his own works, including extracts from *Hugh Selwyn Mauberley*, on the University of Pennsylvania site, **http://writing. upenn.edu/ pennsound**

GLOSSARY

3	**pro domo** for home (Latin)
11–12	**pro patria ... decor** refers to the Latin tag 'Dulce et decorum est pro patria mori' which Owen used; see the glossary for 'Dulce Et Decorum Est', above, for a translation
18	**usury** lending money at a high rate of interest

T. S. ELIOT: TRIUMPHAL MARCH

- Spectators describe an enormous military parade.
- Eventually the leader passes and the procession enters a temple.

A military parade is described from the point of view of spectators in the crowd. A large number of armaments pass by, then various representatives of organisations. Finally the leader, impassive, rides by. The parade moves on to the temple and the watchers clear away their things.

COMMENTARY

Although apparently voicing the observations of the ordinary people who stand in the street to watch the display of armed might, this poem includes fragments of great complexity that point to the poet's wider concerns. The language demonstrates this, including both 'sausages' and 'crumpets' (12 and 46) and a reference to 'the still point of the turning world' (35). This is initially confusing because Eliot deliberately mixes elements from the ancient Rome of history and of Shakespeare, such as the 'eagles' of line 3, and products of modern industry, notably armaments. The opening line demonstrates Eliot's **impressionistic** method, with a list of nouns as though recording the changing images passing the spectators in a stream in front of the stone buildings without any evident coherence. The list, heavily punctuated as it is by commas, gives the line a weighty tone, as if echoing the drum of a band in the procession. At times it seems we are listening to a **monologue**, at

CONTEXT

'Triumphal March' was first published in 1931 as part of the *Ariel Poems* series of pamphlets containing illustrated poems. It appeared later in Eliot's *Collected Poems* under the title *Coriolan*, a reference to Shakespeare's *Coriolanus* in which the central character is hailed as a hero by the people of imperial Rome after a great victory. By 1931 the Italian dictator Mussolini had been in power for several years.

others the questions and answers imply a conversation in the crowd ('What comes first? Can you see? Tell us', 13). The apparently inconsequential topics are also broken into by what appear to be personal reflections on the scene either by the main speaker or by an external **narrator** of a philosophical inclination: 'We hardly knew ourselves that day, or knew the City' (5) implies that something overwhelming was occurring. There is an even greater disjunction in the line, 'The natural wakeful life of our Ego is a perceiving' (11), followed immediately by reference to 'our stools and our sausages' Line 11 contains a quotation from the philosopher Edmund Husserl; it is a feature of Eliot's work to include both the mundane and the esoteric, leaving the reader to puzzle out connections. Here, Eliot follows the quotation by listing in elaborate detail the armaments in the procession – so he is perhaps suggesting that the public's perceptions are easily overwhelmed by a show of force and cowed into accepting those who wield power. The huge numbers make clear that this is not an actual procession (as the mix of ancient and modern features has already implied) but a vision of the destructive machinery that industrialised warfare employs.

When the leader appears he is anonymous and Eliot emphasises that he is 'perceiving, indifferent' (32) – perhaps as much at the mercy of military might and the need to conform to expectations as the spectators are. The next three lines change the focus again; Eliot twice uses an invocation 'O hidden' (33 and 35) but only hints at what is hidden. The two references to doves suggest love, faithfulness, peace and, for Eliot as a Christian, the Holy Spirit in the Trinity, whilst 'the palmtree at noon' (34) suggests rest (though perhaps only temporary) and 'the still point of the turning world' (35) implies that this is a crucial moment in history. The events, however, proceed now to 'the sacrifice' (36) – and the mention of 'virgins bearing urns' (37) suggests some sinister ritual, though again this is only hinted at. Their urns contain dust, implying that all this ceremony is worthless. Eliot hints at something more in the chatter of the crowd at the end, with its reference to 'Easter Day' (44), the central point in the Christian calendar and perhaps therefore Eliot's 'still point' – though the speaker's account reduces this to an incident for which 'young Cyril' (45) shows little respect (just as the adults seemed only to go to church because they 'didn't get to the

CHECK THE BOOK

Eliot wrote: 'The poet must become more and more comprehensive, more allusive, more indirect, in order to force, to dislocate if necessary, language into his meaning' ('The Metaphysical Poets' in *Selected Essays*, 1951).

CHECK THE POEM

The 'still point of the turning world' is a key idea of Eliot's, and is also used in his 'Burnt Norton, Part 2', one of his *Four Quartets* (1935–42): '... at the still point, there the dance is, / But neither arrest nor movement'.

country', 44). Eliot leaves the reader with conflicting images – the request for 'a light' (49) turns into a cry for 'Light / Light' (50–1) as if to reinforce the impression given by the casual comments on the church service that they are in spiritual darkness. Have the crowd become followers of a crowd-pleasing politician rather than Jesus, who said, 'I am the light of the world: he that followeth me shall not walk in darkness' (John's Gospel, 8:12)? Finally, the line in French disorientates the reader again by reintroducing the soldiers. Eliot was one of the main figures in literary **modernism** so it should not be surprising that 'Triumphal March' is fragmentary and **allusive**, portraying an unsettled, disturbing world and hinting at several interpretations.

GLOSSARY

33	**turtle** turtle-dove
52	***Et les soldats … FAISAIENT*** And the soldiers formed the guard of honour? They formed it (French)

RUDYARD KIPLING: EPITAPHS OF THE WAR

- A series of thirty-four epitaphs for a wide variety of men and women who died in the war.

CONTEXT

Following the war Rudyard Kipling became a member of the Imperial (now Commonwealth) War Graves Commission and chose the inscription 'Their name liveth for evermore' for war memorials.

The 'Epitaphs' pay tribute to many categories of people who served during the war, including soldiers from different parts of the British empire, a coward, a sentry who fell asleep on duty, parents, sailors, women, actors and journalists.

COMMENTARY

Kipling's **epitaphs**, like those which would be inscribed on actual graves, are brief tributes to those who contributed to the war and were published in 1919. There is a long tradition of commemoration in this way; after the Battle of Thermopylae in 480 BC, the Greek poet Simonides of Ceos wrote this epitaph to the Spartans who perished there (here in Bowles's translation, which Stallworthy prints on page 9 of *The Oxford Book of War Poetry*): 'Go tell the Spartans, thou that passest by, / That here, obedient to their laws, we lie.'

Often just a **rhyming couplet**, Kipling's 'Epitaphs' address the reader mostly in the voices of the dead, conveying their messages simply and directly. As might be expected of a writer who had sought to capture the voice of the common soldier (see his 'Tommy' on p. 143) and who had lived in India, his cast is made up of ordinary men and women – some heroic, some victims – from across the world. The tone is indicated in the title of the first epitaph: 'Equality of Sacrifice'. Rich and poor have given equally by laying down their lives, so all are equal in death – indeed, 'A Servant' is 'the better man' than his officer in the second epitaph. In this way Kipling raises an issue that he and many others considered as the war progressed: how to give proper dignity to the large numbers of the dead. His work as a member of the Imperial War Graves Commission was another response to this. This concern can be seen in 'The Favour', where death assures the man who has no family to succeed him that he will still be commemorated (as thousands were on war memorials): '"Thy line is at end," he said, "but at least I have saved its name."' At the end of 'The Canadian Memorials' the living are trusted to keep 'that world we won'. In contrast, the solder in 'Pelicans in the Wilderness' has no known grave (the fate of Kipling's own son): in both cases, there is an implicit admonition to the living to preserve their memory and prize the peace they won.

Kipling's dead here are anonymous yet, as he claims for the 'Ex-Clerk', they are 'content' to have served for 'The Army gave / Freedom to a timid slave'. The dead have served different gods, though Kipling seems to view these beliefs from his own (British but not necessarily Christian) point of view: the Hindu Sepoy 'prayed we know not to what Powers'. Death and Fate seem more significant than any specific belief (see 'The Favour' and 'Destroyers in Collision') and to be one of 'The Obedient' seems more important than any creed, although 'the Gods bestowed no gift' and did not protect these victims. Being true to one's own beliefs is valued, even if, as in 'The Refined Man', that means death rather

> **CONTEXT**
>
> Rudyard Kipling was deeply affected by the death in 1915 of his only son John just six weeks after his 18th birthday. Kipling had used his influence to have John accepted into the Army despite his appalling eyesight; his body was never found. Several of the 'Epitaphs' refer to sons and the bitterness of 'Common Form' may in part be directed by Kipling at himself.

CONTEXT

VADs were members of the Voluntary Aid Detachment, an organisation for women who served as auxiliary nurses, ambulance drivers, etc., during the war.

than compromising personal standards. Kipling includes some who had been condemned as well as heroes, implying that as 'The Coward' and 'The Sleepy Sentinel' were part of the story of the war, they too must be remembered. His words convey the **pathos** of the situations of these two men, but not criticism. Women have a place, though mostly it is passive, like the mother in 'An Only Son' or the bride in 'The Bridegroom'. The abused and disfigured women in 'Unknown Female Corpse' and 'Raped and Revenged' are pitied but the main emphasis seems to be on how their deaths are viewed by men ('I beseech all women's sons / Know I was a mother once') or what they show about the difference between the British and 'the heathen' – that is, the brutal enemy. The VAD nurse is celebrated – but again, she is mourned by 'men she nursed'.

Only in a few of the epitaphs does Kipling adopt a **satirical** tone for those who, in his view, have betrayed the dead. Knowing that his own son perished early in the war, it is hard not to read epitaphs such as 'The Beginner' and the several poems that refer to a son, mother or father as poignant tributes to John Kipling or even expressions of guilt – the third Epitaph, 'A Son', is a moving expression of this and, unlike the others, appears to be spoken by the surviving father rather than the dead son. Particularly forceful is the accusatory couplet 'Common Form':

> If any question why we died,
> Tell them, because our fathers lied.

This can be read to mean that 'our fathers' lied to us, the dead, or that you (the reader) must now tell questioners the truth because 'our fathers' lied to the public – either reading is an indictment of the 'old men'. This contrast between the old, who lied, and the young, who died, is reiterated in the lines on 'A Dead Statesman' and echoes the attacks by soldier-poets such as Owen and Sassoon as well as the words Pound was to use a year later in *Hugh Selwyn Mauberley* (see p. 210). Kipling returns to the theme of deception in his final epitaph by giving the journalists (whom the troops universally regarded as liars) only a single line. The **irony** is bitter: unlike those who died in battle, the journalists have 'served' the day by pleasing the public at the expense of truth – now they have served their turn and are no longer wanted.

GLOSSARY

'Equality of Sacrifice'	a 'have-not' someone who is poor
'Hindu Sepoy in France'	**Sepoy** an Indian soldier serving in the British army
'The Rebel'	**gin** trap for animals
'A Drifter off Tarentum'	**drifter** a kind of fishing-boat, here carrying out mine-sweeping duties
	Tarentum the Latin name for the Italian naval port of Taranto

ELIZABETH DARYUSH: SUBALTERNS

- A woman's enthusiastic talk about battle and two officers' subdued reactions.

A woman is excited at the thought of battle; a young officer replies that his memories of combat are chilling. To another she remarks how he must feel free now battle is over; but for him, life now seems dull.

COMMENTARY

Elizabeth Daryush's carefully balanced **stanzas** contrast the thoughtless enthusiasm of the female with the cold reality of the officers' experiences. In the first dialogue, the officer actually feels that his memories cast a chill over the present. The tone of 'battle's glorious throes' (3), with its glib **rhyme** with 'glows' from the first line, contrasts with the heavier, accented tone of 'Are icy memories' (5) and the rhyme with 'freeze' (6) which darkens the 'sunny hours they bought' (7). The second conversation has the same format but here the contrast is not between heat and cold but lightness and heaviness. For the second officer, the war has so shaken him that, like his colleague in the first stanza, life is permanently affected. The tone here is more informal: 'Well, I don't know … ' (11), though the apparently innocuous 'deadly slow' (14) conceals a play on the

CHECK THE POEM

Elizabeth Daryush's sentiments are echoed by Wilfred Owen in 'The Send-Off' (p. 192) as he wonders if the men going off to war 'yet mock what women meant Who gave them flowers'. There are three more of Elizabeth Daryush's poems in *Scars Upon My Heart*.

word 'deadly' that implies that something has been killed inside him by his experience. The rhyme scheme is skilfully crafted to tie each dialogue together and in particular stress the more sombre reactions of the officers.

> ### GLOSSARY
>
> title   **Subalterns** junior officers, below the rank of Captain

MAY WEDDERBURN CANNAN: ROUEN

- A nurse at an army hospital remembers her working day during the war, meeting the trains of wounded and resting in the evening.

The poem describes the life of a nurse at an army hospital in France, moving from dawn, through the morning's work and evenings shared with the soldiers. A group of men leaves; the nurses relax in the town.

COMMENTARY

This poem, first published in 1917, arose from May Wedderburn Cannan's own time in Rouen during the war: the dates at the head of the poem confirm this. Within a highly regulated structure and with a tightly controlled **rhythm** she conveys a vivid impression of the strangeness, excitement and sadness of those few weeks. The mainly **anapaestic** rhythm and the repetitive syntax drive the verse forward in the manner of a lively conversation. The **narrator** draws in the reader by repeated questions, as if addressing a fellow VAD. In all, nine of the thirteen **stanzas** begin 'Can ...' and end with a question mark and three more (the first, third and fifth) have another pattern, stating the time of day 'over Rouen'. Most of the subsequent lines in each stanza begin 'And the ...', which increases the sense of breathless excitement. The tone is set from the start by the use of three **stressed** adjectives filled with optimism at the end of the first

CHECK THE BOOK

May Wedderburn Cannan worked not as a nurse but as a volunteer in the British Army canteen at Rouen for four weeks, serving coffee and sandwiches to the soldiers. The story can be found in Cannan's autobiography, *Grey Ghosts and Voices* (1976).

line: 'hopeful, high, courageous morning'. The language continues to convey enthusiasm in words such as 'laughter' (2), 'wonder' (6), and 'the freshness and the glory of the labour of the day' (8). The **impressionistic** nature of the poem derives partly from Cannan's use of what are essentially a series of lists of sounds and sights appropriate to the time of day she is describing. The stanzas she uses to mark the time of day are not strictly sentences; the lack of a main verb again reinforces the sense of snapshots rather than a narrative. The commitment to the cause is evident in the seventh stanza, where devotion to the men, seen in the parcels the women make for them, is matched by devotion to their country, whatever the 'agony' it might cause, that they feel as they stand for the national anthem: 'And the agony and splendour when they stood to save the King' (28). It is an image of devotion to the country's cause that doubtless inspired many, particularly at the onset of the war (this was in 1915). The images have an air of romantic adventure: 'And the distant call of bugles, and the white wine in the glasses, / And the long line of the street lamps, stretching Eastwards to the sea?' (47–8). It is therefore not surprising that in the final stanza, 'our Adventure' (51) is what the narrator calls her time in Rouen.

CHECK THE BOOK

For a contrasting account of a VAD's experiences, read the novel *Not So Quiet* by Helen Zenna Smith, first published in 1930. Based on a young woman's wartime diary, it recounts the harsh life of an ambulance driver at the French front.

GLOSSARY

12	**tatties** screens over the windows
15	**Woodbines** brand of cigarette
27, 40	**Drafts** group of soldiers selected for a task, posting, etc.

PHILIP LARKIN: MCMXIV

- A description of scenes at the outbreak of war in 1914, as men queue up to enlist.

Men wanting to enlist form long queues in August 1914. The towns and countryside seem unchanged but that world was to disappear for ever.

COMMENTARY

Larkin's poem was first published in 1964, fifty years after the outbreak of hostilities. In it he looks back on Britain in August 1914. His description of this distant time seems detached, as if he is describing a series of old photographs or a primitive film. As always with Larkin, however, this is deceptive; he makes the reader become aware of the significance of the scenes by gradually accumulating telling details until the final **stanza**'s repeated **refrain** tolls for the end of 'innocence'. The poem reads deceptively easily, too; in fact it is crafted with Larkin's usual scrupulous care. Written in one long sentence, it begins with a gesture, indicating something unusual: 'Those long uneven lines'. The next two stanzas continue to build up the picture, each beginning with 'And' until the final stanza marks the total separation of that time from the present with 'Never' repeated twice more.

Larkin selects details that will convey the innocence of the time, knowing his readers will be aware that the people he describes had no idea of the slaughter that was soon to be unleashed upon Europe. The men outside recruiting offices are compared to crowds queuing to watch a cricket or football match, 'an August Bank Holiday lark' (8) that would claim the lives of many of them. The 'long uneven lines' (1) are suggested by the uneven line-lengths in the stanza, where the third line is 'stretched' like the queue. The second stanza emphasises the 'archaic' nature of the scene that he had already mentioned in reference to the men's old-fashioned moustaches (6). The advertisements, the money ('farthings and sovereigns', 11), even the children's names (which he cleverly alludes to without telling us what they were: we need to think of Victoria, George or Edward for ourselves) are all from another world. The same is true of 'the pubs' (15): Larkin probably knew that during the war the Defence of the Realm Act forced licensed premises to close during working hours, but more important is the impression he creates of a public holiday, as if this is a time for celebration rather than fearful anticipation. In the third stanza Larkin alludes to the beauty of the summer countryside, unchanged, he implies, since 'Domesday' (20) but also 'not caring' (17) (and the mention of 'Domesday' introduces a sense that for these people, their day of doom is approaching). The social

CHECK THE BOOK

In Alan Bennett's play *The History Boys* (2004), the history teacher Irwin argues against acceptance of Owen's and Sassoon's view of the war, saying 'try Kipling' (he quotes 'Common Form', p. 216). One boy responds, 'You can't explain away the poetry, sir', and the sixth formers recite from memory the whole of 'MCMXIV'.

order, too, with its 'servants' (22), is doomed. The final stanza is a summary of the judgement of history on that time. 'Never before or since' (26) condenses into four words the widely held view that pre-First World War Britain was uniquely blessed and ignorant at the same time – Larkin seems to have in mind the contrast between the beautiful pre-war summer, with its ordered society and ideals of Empire, and the devastation that fell upon it in the trenches. His detail of the 'tidy' gardens (29) is succeeded by the even more painful reminder that 'thousands of marriages' would last only 'a little while longer' (30–1). His final line rhymes with the fourth line of the stanza (as each final line has) to give a subtle cohesion to the structure. Larkin repeats the first line of the stanza but with the addition of an extra word to lengthen the line and impart a sense of finality. 'Innocence' itself has 'changed itself to past' (27) and no later generation would view the outbreak of war in the same way.

QUESTION

Why do you think Larkin calls the poem 'MCMXIV' and not '1914'?

GLOSSARY

4	**the Oval or Villa Park** respectively, a cricket ground in London, and a football stadium in Birmingham
15	**twist** a kind of pipe tobacco
20	**Domesday lines** the fields follow boundaries recorded in the Doomsday Book of 1086

TED HUGHES: SIX YOUNG MEN

- A description of a photograph of six young men taken on the moors. Each perished in the war.

The **narrator** looks at a photograph of six young men taken forty years previously on the moors at a place he knows well. All died within six months; now this picture is all that is left of them. Knowing what became of them chills the narrator.

COMMENTARY

Ted Hughes introduced this poem at the Adelaide Festival Writers' Week with these words: 'This is a meditation of a kind – on a

CHECK THE POEM

The final poems in the First World War section of *The Oxford Book of War Poetry* are by poets who were born after the war but whose imagination is still held by images of the time. Compare Hughes's response to those of Vernon Scannell in 'The Great War' (p. 223) and Douglas Dunn in 'War Blinded' (p. 225). Stallworthy also includes a poem by Herbert Read, who served in the First War and addressed a poem 'To a Conscript of 1940' (p. 242).

photograph of six youths. And it's taken in a valley just below where I lived in Yorkshire and just before the outbreak of the First World War. These six youths were all friends of my father. And the war came, and this photograph is just one among family photographs – so I've been hearing stories about these characters on this photograph for as long as I've been picking up the photograph and looking at it.' Even without this confirmation from the author of the existence of an actual photograph and a specific location, it is evident that the poem is a meditation on the power of a picture to preserve life and yet remind us vividly of death – both of those in the photograph and our own. The first few lines bring out this tension: the men have not aged in the photograph though it has suffered from the effects of time. Hughes gives the men an artless charm – 'one lowers his eyes, bashful, / One is ridiculous with cocky pride' (7–8) – only to tell us that six months later 'they were all dead' (9). That contrast between life and death features also in the second **stanza**. Where they were photographed is as full of life as ever: 'through all / The leafy valley a rumouring of air go' (14–15) but again the last line reminds us of their fate. Having recounted the deaths in the third stanza Hughes returns to the photograph, now unable to look at it without imagining the tortured last hours of these men; 'this one place which keeps him alive' (33) is also a constant reminder that each man is dead. The final stanza turns the meditation toward the reader: these men are vividly alive in the photograph yet utterly dead, 'Nor prehistoric or fabulous beast more dead' (40). The image of 'their smoking blood' (41) captures both the essence of life and its end in bloodshed, so that we are chilled by this realisation. Hughes's words, 'shoulder out / One's own body from its instant and heat' (44–5) create a disturbing image of death pushing us aside as the conclusion of the poem.

Later in the same talk, Hughes mentioned that he had been 'greatly infatuated' by the poetry of Wilfred Owen. There certainly are some of Owen's traits in this poem, including the heavy **alliteration** on 'f' in lines 2 and 3 and the use of **half-rhymes** such as 'friends'/'hands' (2, 4) and 'pride'/'dead' (8, 9). Hughes's own voice is clear, however, in the sense of the particularity of the flesh, the 'mightier-than-a-man dead bulk and weight' (32). The poem is not just about the First World War; like the skulls that feature in sixteenth- and seventeenth-century paintings, the photograph is a *memento mori* – an object that reminds us that we must all die.

GLOSSARY	
11	**bilberried** covered with bilberry plants, which grow on moorlands
34	**Sunday best** best clothes, normally worn only on Sundays (see line 10)

EXTENDED COMMENTARIES

TEXT 1 – EDWARD THOMAS: AS THE TEAM'S HEAD BRASS

As the ploughing team works its way up and down the field, a soldier talks with the ploughman about the war and how it has claimed a number of the other farm-workers so that the fallen elm on which the soldier sits cannot be cleared away. The soldier has not yet been to the front; he considers the possibility that he could be wounded or even killed. A pair of lovers goes into the wood and returns again as the team start a new furrow.

The bald summary of the poem above indicates that little happens in the rural scene that Thomas describes. However, in these thirty-seven lines he conveys a strong sense of the effect of the war on the rhythms of country life and indeed on all of life. The scene appears to be one of **pastoral** tranquillity; as the horses work their way across the field, with the spring sunlight flashing on the decorative brasses, 'the lovers disappeared into the wood' (2). Yet this traditional, unchanging scene is subtly threatened; the **narrator**, who we come to realise is a soldier awaiting the call to the front line, sits on a 'fallen elm' (3). This hint of destruction recurs in line 7, with its reference to the horses 'treading me down' (as might well happen to him on the battlefield). The pace and structure of the poem are conversational; Thomas makes it clear that they only exchange 'a word' (8) each time the team turns at the end of the furrow, with ten minutes in between. The movement of the poem is therefore shaped by the movement of the plough up and down

CHECK THE BOOK

Bernard Bergonzi writes of 'As the team's head brass': 'In bare and direct lines he evokes both the permanence of human love and human labour, and, in the pregnant words, "for the last time", the transience of the moment' (*Heroes' Twilight*, Carcanet, 1996, p. 81).

the field. Thomas, like the poet Robert Frost (see p. 169) who had encouraged him to take up poetry, writes in **free verse** but the style is carefully crafted, as a study of the ways he runs sentences across lines will reveal. The little pause at the end of line 7 ('ploughman leaned / Upon the handles') catches the pause as the horses turn. By lines 30–1 the breaks indicate the magnitude of the changes brought by the war: 'Everything / Would have been different.'

'The war' is mentioned in the same way as the weather – like the 'blizzard' that 'felled the elm' (13), it has brought its troubles to the farm by killing a number of the workers so the fallen tree cannot be cleared till 'the war's over' (16). Even here, the tone seems matter-of-fact: 'One of my mates is dead. The second day / In France they killed him' (26–7). More chilling is the dispassionate way the soldier assesses the risks he faces: 'I could spare an arm. I shouldn't want to lose / A leg. If I should lose my head, why, so, / I should want nothing more' (21–3). The placing of 'a leg' on the next line gives the reader a jolt. The soldier's wry joke in the next sentence, as if losing his head were no different to losing a limb, is also **ambiguous**. In a poem by Brooke, this would imply the nobility of patriotic sacrifice – here it merely seems to be a recognition that he will indeed 'want nothing more' once he is dead. This ambiguity continues in line 33: 'If we could see all all might seem good.' The repetition of 'all' in the middle of the line feels awkward but the pause it forces on the reader emphasises the difficulty of weighing up what is really 'good'. Is it 'good' for the soldier to go to war and perhaps die for his country? Thomas implies that because we cannot 'see all' we have no way of knowing.

The poem ends with a reminder of the lovers, who come into view again. Yet even they, who could be taken as signifying hope, seem threatened by the context, coming as they do between the uncertainty of knowing the future and the words 'for the last time' in line 35. It may be the last turn of the plough across the field but it might also be the 'last time' for the lovers and for the soldier if the war strikes them. The final two words confirm this sense of foreboding, with the word 'stumbling', as if neither horses nor humans can find their way.

QUESTION

Compare Thomas's rural scene to the one in Hardy's 'In Time of "The Breaking of Nations"' (p. 161). Both refer to the cycles of country life and each includes a pair of lovers. How do they differ in their response to war? What is the effect, do you think, of the fact that Hardy wrote at the very start of the war and Thomas half-way through?

GLOSSARY

1	head-brass the horse brasses of the ploughing team: brass decorations mounted on leather that hang in the middle of the horses' heads
4	fallow a field left uncultivated for a year
6	charlock a yellow-flowered weed
10	share ploughshare, the blade that turns over the soil

TEXT 2 – ISAAC ROSENBERG: BREAK OF DAY IN THE TRENCHES

The **narrator**, a soldier on duty in the early morning, picks a poppy from the parapet, disturbing a rat as he does so. He muses on the reversal of normality: the rat is free to pass between the English and German lines whilst strong men are likely to die attempting to make the same journey. He wonders what the rat sees in the eyes of soldiers under fire. Meanwhile, he says, the poppy, although covered with a little dust, is safe behind his ear.

Like many of Rosenberg's poems, this captures a fleeting moment and reflects on its significance. It moves from the quiet, understated description of the soldier picking a poppy and disturbing a rat to reflect on the **irony** of the situation in which a rat is freer, and safer, than a fit young man. The final section, from line 19, introduces a more violent note as it imagines the rat watching the men under bombardment by 'shrieking iron and flame / Hurled through still heavens' (20–1) before returning to the image of the poppy behind his ear, apparently 'safe' (25). The rat that 'leaps' in his hand (3) is full of life and 'sardonic' (4) because Rosenberg attributes to the creature mockery at the situation of these 'haughty athletes' (14) who, unlike the rat, cannot pass freely across No Man's Land, the seemingly innocuous 'sleeping green' (12). The situation is lent extra irony by the fact that 'break of day' (like dusk) was marked on both sides by 'stand-to', when all troops stood up to the firing step with rifles loaded and bayonets fixed, tensely peering across for signs of the enemy since these were the most likely times for an attack. (It was far removed from the romantic associations of dawn, as Paul Fussell points out in his section on 'Sunrise and Sunset' in

CONTEXT

A version of the poem appears to have been completed by Rosenberg about a month after arriving at the front. He wrote to Edward Marsh on 6 August 1916: 'I am enclosing a poem I wrote in the trenches, which is surely as simple as ordinary talk. You might object to the second line as vague, but that was the best way I could express the sense of dawn.'

QUESTION

What do you think Rosenberg means by 'the same old druid Time' in the second line of the poem?

CHECK THE POEM

Another poem which includes both rats and a poppy is Herbert Asquith's 'After the Salvo' (*Up the Line to Death*, p. 81). Asquith too comments on the irony that 'man's house is crushed; the spider lives', though the rats are shot at the end of his poem.

CHECK THE NET

Oxford University's First World War Poetry Digital Archive provides an annotated copy of 'Break of Day in the Trenches' and a rich set of links about the historical and literary context. See **www.ww1lit.com**

Chapter 2 of *The Great War and Modern Memory*, Oxford, 1975.) In the poem's title, day *breaks*: this suggests a fracture, destruction, as does 'crumbles' in line 1.

In this situation of imminent danger, the grinning rat can be 'cosmopolitan' (8) as no soldier can; Rosenberg makes this plain by imagining the rat touching first an 'English hand' and then a German one (9–10), with the alteration of **stress** in these two lines suggesting the easy movement of the creature across the lines and nationalities, which are placed at the end of each line to emphasise their opposition. This careful balancing occurs again in lines 14 and 15; the pairs of words emphasise the vitality of the men three times: 'Strong eyes, fine limbs, haughty athletes' – yet the word 'haughty' implies the folly of this perception, as the cool statement of the next line makes clear. The word 'life' at the end of that line is matched and refuted by 'murder' at the end of the following one. Rosenberg imagines he sees the rat 'grin' (13) at the situation; rather than a creature at the mercy of men, it is the rat who observes their fear, which he expresses in the two questions of line 22. Whilst the rat watches, 'still heavens' (21) could be taken to imply that there are no divine powers to intervene, only rats – and men whose destruction is worse than animals because less logical.

Rosenberg returns to the poppy in the final lines, an even more evocative **symbol** of the trenches than the ever-present rat. At the beginning of the poem, wearing the poppy seemed an affirmation of life, a carefree gesture; now its significance is more sombre. 'Poppies whose roots are in man's veins' (23) recalls the common association of poppies and the fallen by making it explicit, so that they seem to drink the blood from the very bodies of the dead. The next line is potently ambiguous; the poppies '[d]rop, and are ever dropping' but the words also sound as though they apply to the men – as, of course, they do. For the safety of the poppy is illusory – it is already 'white with the dust' (26) of death, not just the dust of a trench in summer. ('Dust' has long been **synonymous** with death; in the Old Testament, God says to Adam: 'Dust thou art, and unto dust shalt thou return', Genesis 3:19. The Church of England burial service uses a similar formulation: 'Earth to earth, ashes to ashes, dust to dust.') The repeated 'pop' sounds in lines 23 and 24 could even be an ominous echo of machine-gun fire to bring home the point that neither poppy nor soldier will survive for long.

GLOSSARY

5	**parapet** the bank, usually made of sandbags, at the front of the trench to protect soldiers from enemy fire

---

TEXT 3 – WILFRED OWEN: STRANGE MEETING

Owen probably completed this poem just before returning to France for the last time on 31 August 1918. The **narrator**, a soldier, appears to escape from battle into a huge tunnel filled with sleepers. One jumps up and recognises him; he realises the place is 'Hell' (10). The 'other' (15) describes how, had he lived, he would have moved many men with his account of war; now he is dead, humanity will continue its descent into savagery. In one draft, Owen wrote, 'I was a German conscript, and your friend'. In the final version, this becomes 'I am the enemy you killed, my friend' (40), giving the situation a greater universality as well as providing the powerful **oxymoron** that his enemy is now his friend – but only after death.

The **narrative** has a nightmarish quality, from the uncertain opening ('It seemed ... ') to the final suggestion of 'sleep' (44). Sleep in this 'sullen hall' (9) is likely to be troubled; it is a place where 'sleepers groaned' (4). Although the realities of war are distant, it is present both in the situation that has brought these two together and in the way its vocabulary informs the whole poem. Blood soaks the earth, guns still 'thumped' and 'made moan' overhead (13). The man he meets is described as a 'vision' (11), as though to emphasise the unreal nature of this afterlife. He is still suffering, however, 'Lifting distressful hands' (8) and marked 'with a thousand pains' (11); the word 'Yet' at the opening of the second **stanza** stresses that even here the men suffer just as men suffer on the battlefield. When the narrator seeks to console the man he meets, the other's response is resigned but has an undertone of bitterness. He describes what he might have achieved in words rich with the imagery of **Romantic** poetry – the kind of poetry that Owen himself had earlier aspired to

---

CONTEXT

Owen wrote in his draft preface for a collection of war poems that he planned to publish in 1919: 'My subject is War, and the pity of War. The Poetry is in the pity. Yet these elegies are to this generation in no sense consolatory. They may be to the next. All a poet can do today is warn. That is why the true Poets must be truthful.' In his draft 'Table of Contents' for his poems, Owen put alongside this poem: 'Motive: Foolishness of War'.

CHECK THE POEM

The title and subject of the poem are taken from Canto V of Shelley's *The Revolt of Islam* (1817), in which a soldier confronts the enemies who have killed his colleagues and declares: 'We are all brethren.'

CHECK THE BOOK

Susan Hill used Owen's title for her novel *Strange Meeting*, published in 1971; the 'meeting' is the friendship that forms between two British officers, Hilliard and Barton.

write. '[T]he wildest beauty in the world' (18) is not to be found, it seems, in physical beauty ('eyes, or braided hair', 19). Owen appears to have in mind something like the **Romantic** ideal of the sublime, a beauty which by its permanence 'mocks the steady running of the hour' (20) and is eternal. The word 'richlier' (21) is, in its strangeness, a reminder of Owen's love of Keats, and the soldier's words echo Keats in the conclusion to 'Ode on a Grecian Urn': 'Beauty is truth, truth beauty.' For the soldier, too, sought to tell 'the truth untold, / The pity of war' (24–5) and that is now another casualty of war. For beauty 'grieves' (21), that is, it makes us grieve at the destruction and loss war causes. Instead of being moved by the 'truth' that the soldier would have told, 'men will go content with what we spoiled' (26) and will be 'swift' (28) but terrible in destruction. Owen uses his **half-rhyme** to link the 'swiftness of the tigress' (27) with the 'trek from progress' (28) and thus emphasise how the war has destroyed any optimism that the pre-war generation might have had about human progress. Now there is only 'the march of this retreating world' (32), 'blood' (34) and, perhaps worse, the destruction of men's minds that 'have bled where no wounds were' (39).

The second **stanza**, with its account of the ambitions of the dead soldier, has recourse in places to the rich language of nineteenth-century poetry and the Bible, with 'braided hair' (19), 'vain citadels' (33), 'chariot-wheels' (34) and 'the cess of war' (38). The epilogue, which takes us back to the two men, is much more direct, with the force of 'jabbed and killed' reminding us of the grim reality of combat (42). The poem does not so much conclude as break off, with the final half-line ending in ellipsis. Does this mean that the poem offers consolation and hope of reconciliation? The composer Benjamin Britten seemed to think so, setting 'Strange Meeting' at the end of his *War Requiem* of 1962, with the voices of tenor and baritone, representing the two soldiers, singing together 'Let us sleep now … ' whilst a chorus floats the 'In paradisum' of the Latin Mass, ending quietly on 'Requiescant in pace. Amen' ('Let them rest in peace. Amen'). Jon Silkin disagrees: 'I believe the poem does not end optimistically, despite the reconciliation … Owen implies, rather, that although there is reconciliation in death, that is the only place where it can be achieved' (*Out of Battle*, p. 241). To come to a decision, the reader needs to consider whether the final 'sleep' (44) means that the message, the 'truth' about 'the pity of war' and the truth that might 'wash' (35) away all the injury is now to be lost, abandoning humanity to continue on its suicidal path. The best conclusion may be the words of Owen's draft preface: 'All a poet can do today is warn.'

 QUESTION

GLOSSARY	
3	**titanic** colossal
3	**groined** in a building, a 'groin' is the joining place of two vaults in a roof

The poet Michael Roberts writes: 'In Owen's war poetry, the half-rhymes almost invariably fall from a vowel of high pitch to one of low pitch, producing an effect of frustration, disappointment, hopelessness' (*Faber Book of Modern Verse*, 1st edn, 1936). Do you think this is the case here? Do the half-rhymes have other effects, such as intensifying the dream-like quality of this poem?

PART THREE

CRITICAL APPROACHES

THEMES

Studying any anthology, particularly one with as diverse a range of poets as *The Oxford Book of War Poetry*, is likely to introduce a wide range of themes. If we include Douglas Dunn, who was born in 1942 and whose 'War Blinded' on page 225 is about a man who lost his sight sixty years earlier in the First World War, more than one hundred years separate the first poet, Hardy (born in 1840), from the last. This means that the approaches, attitudes and styles of the poems are bound to cover a wide range. The headings here indicate a few of the connections between poems in Stallworthy's selection; as you read and reread you should look out for further links and contrasts.

PATRIOTISM

The outbreak of war in 1914 was accompanied by an outpouring of patriotic enthusiasm that is difficult for modern readers to comprehend, knowing what we do of the subsequent course of the war and of the literature that has come to define it. Philip Larkin makes this a central aspect of his poem 'MCMXIV', commenting: 'Never such innocence again' (p. 222, l. 32). Yet, as Larkin also notes, men enlisted in their thousands during those early months of the war and the fervent patriotism of Rupert Brooke, Julian Grenfell and Herbert Asquith was clearly shared by a wide public. The most famous of these expressions is Brooke's 'The Soldier', which was originally called 'The Recruit' and seems to be fired by the kind of innocence that Larkin mentions. It is enough for Brooke's soldier that death in defence of his country will sanctify his grave and make 'some corner of a foreign field ... for ever England' (p. 163, ll. 2–3). This willing sacrifice is described again in Asquith's 'The Volunteer', in which the dead soldier is seen as joining 'the men of Agincourt' (p. 163, l. 16) – heroes, that is, of a historic, mythologised victory against the odds on foreign soil. Laurence Binyon's 'For the Fallen' is also devoted to the dead and, like Asquith and Brooke, he imagines them exalted into some kind

CHECK THE POEM

For further poems urging men to enlist, see 'The Call' and 'England to Her Sons' by W. N. Hodgson in *Up the Line to Death*, pp. 9f, and Jessie Pope's 'The Call' in *Scars Upon My Heart*, p. 88.

of heaven: 'As the stars that shall be bright when we are dust'
(p. 209, l. 25). Hardy was stirred by the declaration of war to praise
the 'Men Who March Away', calling those who stay 'dalliers' who
do not see that 'England's need are we' (p. 160, ll. 17–18). Like the
other poets, it seems natural to Hardy to use England, rather than
Britain, such were the resonances of this national name (despite the
fact that regiments from the whole of Britain and the Empire were
fighting in Europe).

The patriotism in May Wedderburn Cannan's 'Rouen' is less
strident. When she comments on 'the agony and splendour when
they stood to save the King' (p. 220, l. 28) she would appear to be as
much moved by the bravery of the men and the knowledge that
they would shortly be facing death as by the singing of the national
anthem ('God Save the King'). As she later commented, 'I did not
believe the dead had died for nothing.' In wartime, patriotism is
called upon not only to encourage service of one's own country but
also antagonism towards the enemy. The Canadian doctor John
McCrae is explicit about this in his poem 'In Flanders Fields': the
dead urge the living to '[t]ake up our quarrel with the foe' (p. 165,
l. 10). More nationalist belligerence is evident in other poems,
including many by Jessie Pope that appeared in newspapers and
magazines; in 'The Call' she asks, 'Who'll earn the Empire's thanks
– / Will you, my laddie?' In 1914, Kipling, whose First World War
poetry is represented in *The Oxford Book of War Poetry* only by his
post-war 'Epitaphs', wrote in 'For All We Have and Are' that 'The
Hun is at the gate!' (thereby associating Germany with the
barbarian tribe, the Huns), appealed for 'iron sacrifice' and
concluded, 'Who dies if England live?'

Yet, even at that stage, a poet such as Isaac Rosenberg was voicing
doubts about the war in the conclusion of 'On Receiving News of
the War', which he wrote in 1914 whilst in Cape Town. He sees that
war might '[give] back this universe / Its pristine bloom' (p. 183,
ll. 19–20), which sounds rather like the 'swimmers into cleanness
leaping' in Brooke's 'Peace' (p. 162, l. 4) – but he also describes it as
an 'ancient crimson curse!' (p. 183, l. 17). In 'August 1914',
Rosenberg sees the war as disfiguring: 'A fair mouth's broken tooth'
(p. 183, l. 12).

 CHECK THE NET
You can find
quotations from
May Wedderburn
Cannan's
autobiography,
together with a
photograph of her
from the 1920s, on
the website
**http://aspirations.
english.cam.ac.uk**.
Click on 'Search'
and type the poet's
name into the
searchbox.

PATRIOTISM continued

CONTEXT

The poet May
Wedderburn
Cannan wrote in
her autobiography,
*Grey Ghosts and
Voices*: 'A saying
went round,
"Went to the war
with Rupert
Brooke and came
home with
Siegfried
Sassoon". I had
much admired
some of Sassoon's
verse but I was not
coming home with
him. Someone
must go on
writing for those
who were still
convinced of the
right of the cause
for which they had
taken up arms. I
did not believe the
dead had died for
nothing, nor that
we should have
"kept out of the
war" – the dead
had kept faith,
and so, if we did
not grudge it, had
we.'

As the war progressed, appeals to patriotism began to sound hollow. Wilfred Owen denounced '[t]he old Lie' of 'Dulce et decorum est / Pro patria mori' in his poem 'Dulce Et Decorum Est' (p. 188, ll. 27–8), and Pound wrote contemptuously of 'old men's lies' in *Hugh Selwyn Mauberley* (p. 210, l. 14). Poets wrote of the common experiences that all soldiers, whatever their nationality, shared: the bitter cold of 'Hauptmann Kälte, Colonel Cold' in Rickword's poem 'Winter Warfare' (p. 200, l. 15); the 'cosmopolitan' rat that runs from Rosenberg's hand 'to a German' in 'Break of Day in the Trenches' (p. 184, ll. 8–10); and the death that finally unites them in Owen's 'Strange Meeting'. In that poem, the words 'I am the enemy you killed, my friend' signal the irrelevance of patriotism (p. 193, l. 40). The Irish poet W. B. Yeats also conveyed indifference to the quarrels of the opposing armies in 'An Irish Airman Foresees His Death'. Both literally and **metaphorically**, his airman rises above such nationalisms: 'Those that I fight I do not hate, / Those that I guard I do not love' (p. 174, ll. 3–4). Yeats reflects a different patriotism in 'Easter 1916'; here the heroes he names have given their lives in service of Irish nationalism in opposition to England. He recognises the cost of this, saying 'a terrible beauty is born' (p. 171, l. 16).

As the war dragged on and the cost in both human and financial terms rose, even loyal patriots became critical of the way the war was being conducted. Whilst G. K. Chesterton in his 'Elegy in a Country Churchyard' mourns those 'that fought for England' (p. 212, l. 5) , he concludes with an attack on those in power:

> And they that rule in England
> In stately conclave met,
> Alas, alas for England
> They have no graves as yet. (p. 212, ll. 9–12)

HEROISM

In his introduction to *The Oxford Book of War Poetry*, Jon Stallworthy comments on the persistence of the **chivalric** tradition, in which heroism was allied to a code of honour, courtesy and 'Christian knighthood'. By the end of the nineteenth century this was being challenged by a greater concern for the realities of the suffering soldier, seen in Walt Whitman's 'Beat! Beat! Drums!' and other poems from the American Civil War of 1861–5 (pp. 121–7) and Thomas Hardy's portrayals of the effects of the Boer War of 1899–1902 in 'Drummer Hodge' and 'A Wife in London' (pp. 149–50). The response of many poets to the outbreak of war was, however, to turn once again to the language and **imagery** of the past. Rupert Brooke's 'The Dead' (p. 162) begins with the sounds of antiquity, 'Blow out, you bugles, over the rich Dead!', and refers to 'the red / Sweet wine of youth' (ll. 4–5) and the personified qualities of 'Holiness', 'Love', 'Pain', 'Honour' and 'Nobleness' (ll. 10–13). Herbert Asquith, in 'The Volunteer', manages in five lines to invoke 'lance', 'tournament', 'the gleaming eagles of the legions', 'horsemen' and a medieval banner, 'the oriflamme' (p. 163, ll. 3–7). Julian Grenfell's 'Into Battle' is also full of heroic idealism, with its reference to 'joy of battle' (p. 164, l. 37) and the appeal to a code of honour that declares 'he is dead who will not fight' (l. 7). A. E. Housman turned the insult that the British were 'an Army of Mercenaries' into an occasion to praise those whose 'shoulders held the sky suspended' (p. 167, l. 5) like heroes of classical antiquity. Even David Jones, whose *In Parenthesis* conveys the confusion of modern battle, ennobles his common soldiers by comparing them to figures from British and Welsh myths, classical legends and the Bible (p. 205). Probably the best-remembered poem of the war is Laurence Binyon's 'For the Fallen' – the fourth **stanza** is recited annually at Remembrance Day ceremonies – in which he declares that the heroes 'fell with their faces to the foe' (p. 209, l. 12).

? QUESTION

Of the various portrayals of heroism in the poetry of the First World War, which do you find most effective and why?

The effect of these descriptions, at least for the modern reader, is to distance the conflict and surround it with a halo of romance (in the sense of exciting adventures of chivalrous heroes) that jars with the impression given by most of the First World War poems in the selection. Ivor Gurney's officer in 'The Silent One' is '[a] noble fool, faithful to his stripes' whose life 'ended' straight away (p. 182, l. 5); the private 'politely' declines the order to follow and take 'chance of death, after tearing of clothes' (ll. 11–13); for him, survival is more important than heroism. Owen and Sassoon provide copious reactions to this tradition. Rather than glorious sacrifice, men 'die as cattle' (in Owen's 'Anthem for Doomed Youth', p. 188, l. 1); and the dead soldier in Sassoon's 'The Hero' was actually a 'cold-footed, useless swine' (p. 176, l. 13). Robert Graves comments sardonically on this view of war from the perspective of twenty years later in 'Recalling War': 'Never was such antiqueness of romance' (p. 195, l. 23). Edmund Blunden adopts a similar tone in 'Report on Experience', in which 'honour' is 'taken' not won:

> I have been young, and now am not too old;
> And I have seen the righteous forsaken,
> His health, his honour and his quality taken.
>   This is not what we were formerly told. (p. 199, ll. 1–4)

By the time E. E. Cummings was writing 'my sweet old etcetera', his mother's hope 'that / i would die etcetera / bravely of course' is treated **satirically** (p. 201, ll. 13–15). For Cummings, Olaf (in 'i sing of Olaf glad and big'), who is 'a conscientious object-or' (p. 202, l. 3) and therefore refuses to fight, is the real hero: 'more brave than me:more blond than you' (l. 42).

WAR AND NATURE

One First World War recruiting poster, headed with the title 'Your Country's Call', shows rolling hills, thatched cottages with flowers in bloom and pigeons flocking to the dovecote. A soldier in a kilt, looking slightly incongruous in such an English country scene, gestures to the words: 'Isn't this worth fighting for? Enlist now'. Despite the fact that many of the volunteers would have come from towns and cities, the appeal of an idealised English countryside is echoed in many First World War poems. As Paul Fussell points out in the chapter on 'Arcadian Recourses' in his *The Great War and Modern Memory*, this is part of a long **pastoral** tradition in English literature. Blunden's 'Vlamertinghe: Passing the Château' (p. 199) demonstrates this by opening with a quotation from Keats, 'And all her silken flanks with garlands drest', but ends by noting the **ironic** contrast between the beauty of the 'poppies by the million; / Such damask! such vermilion!' (ll. 11–12) and the likely 'sacrifice' of the men (l. 2), commenting by addressing the reader with the vernacular 'mate': 'But if you ask me, mate, the choice of colour / Is scarcely right; this red should have been much duller' (ll. 13–14).

Hardy, writing 'In Time of "The Breaking of Nations"' at the outset of the war, saw nature as unchanging, unaffected by 'War's annals'

www. CHECK
THE NET
You can find First World War posters on a number of websites; there is a useful selection in the section 'Propaganda Posters' on the First World War website, **www. firstworldwar. com**

(p. 161, l. 11). Edward Thomas seems less convinced that the natural world will emerge unscathed from the war, although 'As the team's head brass' describes a similar scene to Hardy's. His horses are 'stumbling' too but, by placing the word at the end of his poem, Thomas reinforces the uncertainty of the future (p. 180, l. 37). For Julian Grenfell, the birds urge the warrior to 'be swift and keen as they' in 'Into Battle' (p. 164, l. 25), and by anthropomorphising the creatures he enlists them into his heroic purpose. Gurney, in 'To His Love', begs nature to offer instead the consolation of 'masses of memoried flowers' to cover the dead body (p. 181, l. 18).

For soldiers at the front, nature offered glimpses of beauty but could also, especially in winter, be dangerous, as Owen describes in 'Exposure', where bullets are 'less deathly than the air that shudders black with snow' (p. 189, l. 17). Robert Frost observes in 'Range-Finding' how a bullet disturbed nature 'Before it stained a single human breast' (p. 169, l. 3). For Rosenberg the larks' songs bring 'strange joy' in 'Returning, We Hear the Larks' (p. 187, l. 7) but also remind the men that 'Death could drop from the dark / As easily as song' (ll. 10–11). Carl Sandburg sees nature as less caring; although he makes grass the **narrator** of his poem 'Grass' (p. 168), it is merely concerned to cover the bodies as it has with all other scenes of slaughter.

CHECK THE POEM
The image of barbed wire as 'iron' or 'rusty' brambles occurs in a number of poems: compare the way Edmund Blunden uses this image in 'The Zonnebeke Road' (p. 198) with David Jones (*In Parenthesis*, p. 202) and Vernon Scannell in 'The Great War' (p. 223).

The most lasting image of the First World War is the poppy. Adopted as the **symbol** of remembrance by the Royal British Legion in response to McCrae's poem 'In Flanders Fields' (p. 165), the poppy has come to signify the millions who lost their lives in the war. For Blunden in 'Vlamertinghe' (p. 199), their beauty is indeed a symbol of the bloodshed, though he is not grateful for the reminder that soon it could be his blood that is nourishing the flowers. Isaac Rosenberg picks a poppy in 'Break of Day in the Trenches'; like the soldier, it is already sprinkled with the 'dust' of death (p. 184, l. 26). Rosenberg, although he could not have known of the way the poppy would be used after the war, is fully aware that poppies' 'roots are in man's veins' (l. 23). He was no more 'safe' than the poppy was behind his ear (l. 25).

<table>
<tr><td>

CONTEXT

The willingness of people to believe in the supernatural during the war is vividly illustrated by the incident of the 'Angels of Mons'. Arthur Machen's story *The Bowmen*, about how phantom bowmen from the Battle of Agincourt come to the aid of the British troops during the Battle of Mons, appeared in a newspaper in September 1914. It was soon accepted as a true account, despite the author's protestations, with several 'witnesses' reporting seeing the 'angels'.

</td><td>

VISIONS AND DREAMS

At a time of such widespread death, it is not surprising that visions, dreams, premonitions and superstitions were common amongst the troops and their families and reflected in the poetry of the First World War. Whilst poets such as Binyon took comfort in traditional beliefs about a heavenly reward for the 'glorious dead', others recount more troubled dreams and visions. Binyon's sonorous line in 'For the Fallen' states: 'To the innermost heart of their own land they are known' (p. 209, l. 23); his vision has the kind of generality that enables those of any faith or none to assent to this promise of eternal remembrance. Brooke's mention, in 'The Soldier', of the dead being '[a] pulse in the eternal mind' (p. 163, l. 10) has a similar quality and can be linked to Grenfell's assertion that '[a]ll the bright company of Heaven' welcome the warrior in 'Into Battle' (p. 164, l. 15). Charles Sorley offers a much less comforting picture in 'When you see millions of the mouthless dead', rejecting the idea of the dead being recognisable by the living so that anyone who imagines they see a loved one should realise that 'It is a spook … / Great death has made all his for evermore' (p. 167, ll. 13–14).

Several poems reflect on the role of fate. Ivor Gurney's 'Ballad of the Three Spectres' is a grim picture in which the spectres appear to have an agonising future in store; the soldier's 'one–two–three' seems to be a superstitious counting down to this fate as well as military drill (p. 181, l. 18). Edmund Blunden's 'Two Voices' (p. 197) recounts officers commenting 'There's something in the air' (l. 1) and 'We're going South, man' (l. 7) – both of which could be premonitions of death, even though 'the apple-trees [are] all bloom and scent' (l. 12). In such times, some also questioned their religious faith. John Peale Bishop, in 'In the Dordogne', describes soldiers who imagine their courage will be rewarded by the Virgin and Child whose statue they pass as they leave the château where they are billeted – but all that happens is 'each day one died or another' (p. 203, l. 22). Owen's 'Futility' complains to the heavens at the death of a young soldier, crying that if this is the result of creation, why bother? 'O what made fatuous sunbeams toil / To break earth's sleep at all?' (p. 193, ll. 13–14).

</td></tr>
</table>

Isaac Rosenberg asks a similar **rhetorical** question in 'Dead Man's Dump' as he contemplates where the souls of the dead have gone: 'Earth! have they gone into you?' (p. 185, l. 21). Rosenberg implies that their souls will go no further than into the ground, which makes the final, repeated questions at the end of the fourth **stanza** all the more terrible:

> And flung on your hard back
> Is their souls' sack,
> Emptied of God-ancestralled essences.
> Who hurled them out? Who hurled? (ll. 23–6)

It is clear that he blames mankind for this slaughter – and behind that is the further question: 'To what purpose was 'the wild honey of their youth' drained from these men (l. 31)? Owen is more reflective in 'Strange Meeting'; although he describes the setting of the poem as 'Hell' (p. 193, l. 10), it appears to allow the spirits of Owen's soldiers to converse and even to 'sleep' at the end of the poem (l. 44). It is, however, a place of sadness, of regret and perhaps, finally, of despair since the speaker knows that the message he would have told will now not reach humanity:

> ... I mean the truth untold,
> The pity of war, the pity war distilled.
> Now men will go content with what we spoiled,
> Or, discontent, boil bloody, and be spilled. (ll. 24–7)

In Owen's vision it seems that the future holds only the prospect of more war, rather than this being 'the war to end wars'.

STRUCTURE

Stallworthy writes in his introduction that 'the poems [in *The Oxford Book of War Poetry*] … have, with few exceptions, been arranged chronologically by conflict' (p. xxx). This is relatively easy to follow, even though he provides no signposts in the body of the text. He begins the First World War section with two poems by Hardy from the outbreak of the war, followed by three of Brooke's famous '1914' **sonnet** sequence. The poems continue in roughly the order of composition, at least with the first poem Stallworthy has

CHECK THE BOOK

Ernest Hemingway's semi-autobiographical novel, *A Farewell to Arms* (1929), is one of the most famous prose responses to the War. It tells the story of Lieutenant Frederic Henry, an American soldier serving as an ambulance driver in Italy. It shares to some degree Owen's bleak outlook.

QUESTION

What further themes seem to you to be important in the First World War poems in this selection? You might like to consider aspects such as the machinery of war, class distinctions (officers and men, etc.), truth and lies, remembrance and commemoration.

selected by each writer. Therefore Yeats's poems on the Easter Rising of 1916 come quite early in the First World War selection although they are followed by two on the death of Major Robert Gregory, even though the second of these, 'Reprisals', dates from 1920 when the war is over and demobilised British soldiers – 'half-drunk or whole-mad soldiery' (p. 175, l. 15) – are terrorising the Irish countryside. This means that it is possible to see the development of what is now accepted as the conventional **narrative** of First World War poetry: the increasingly **realistic**, critical, bitter and **satirical** depiction of the war.

QUESTION

In which other ways could you organise the poems in the selection?

There are some inconsistencies, however: Binyon's deeply traditional lament 'For the Fallen', written in September 1914 (p. 209), comes after the satirical protest of E. E. Cummings against empty war rhetoric in 'next to of course god america i' and his celebration of the 'conscientious object-or' Olaf (p. 202). Binyon's poem is in turn followed immediately by Pound's *Hugh Selwyn Mauberley* in which Pound complains even more bitterly than Cummings about 'old men's lies' and writes of his disgust that at the end of the war, soldiers 'came home ... to old lies and new infamy' (p. 210, ll. 15–17). Towards the end of the First World War selection, Kipling's 'Epitaphs of the War' (p. 213) provide some kind of overview of the extent of the war (and the only real references to theatres of war outside the Western Front, such as conflict in the Middle East and at sea). Stallworthy concludes the selection with four post-war poets – in fact, these poems all date from after the Second World War, as Vernon Scannell makes explicit in 'The Great War' (p. 223). Their perspective is bound to be different, concerned as they are not with first-hand experience of the war but with how it affected others and how, in Douglas Dunn's words in 'War Blinded', that 'story's troubled me' (p. 225, l. 5).

POETIC FORM

As might be expected there is a wide variety of poetic form in the selection, from traditional to experimental. It is not surprising that Thomas Hardy, born in 1840, should sound like a Victorian poet, nor that many others wrote in traditional forms and styles, for many of the 'soldier poets' had hardly left school before they were in uniform and, under the pressure of the moment, sought to capture their experiences in the ways they had studied at their (mostly public) schools. This can be seen in the work of Wilfred Owen, even in the small sample in *The Oxford Book of War Poetry*. This begins with a **sonnet**, 'Anthem for Doomed Youth', rich in the language of Keats and later **Romanticism** (p. 188); by the time of 'Strange Meeting' (p. 193) his writing is much more experimental, with **free-verse** style and **half-rhymes**. Brooke and Sorley also wrote sonnets – but so did the **modernist** E. E. Cummings, whose rejection of the rules of punctuation and an unusual word-break hide the sonnet form in 'next to of course god america i' (p. 202). Ivor Gurney uses the **ballad** form in 'Ballad of the Three Spectres' (p. 181), perhaps implying a link to the superstitions of the past. Kipling shows in his 'Epitaphs of the War' (p. 213) how the same form, often just two lines long, can be used for a wide variety of effects, from the **pathos** of 'A Son' and the celebration of the ordinary man in 'A Servant' to the wry humour of 'A Grave Near Cairo', the social comment on workers at home in 'Batteries Out of Ammunition' and the savage satire of 'Common Form'.

A number of poets found free verse gave them greater scope to express the new experiences of the war; Sassoon in 'The Rear-Guard' (p. 177) and Rosenberg in 'Break of Day in the Trenches' (p. 184) both show how the form gives greater flexibility. The American writers Carl Sandburg and Wallace Stevens use terse free-verse forms to express the indifference of the world to the deaths of soldiers. Even more experimental are the forms used by the French poets Benjamin Péret and particularly Guillaume Apollinaire with his **calligram** in the shapes of star and cannon (pp. 170–1). They are examples of the kinds of European modernism that was only just beginning to affect writing in England in the years before the war. Two more American writers, Ezra Pound and T. S. Eliot, were living in England in 1914 and were both highly influential modernists. Their poems (pp. 210–12) were written after the war and in their fragmented style express the disillusionment felt and a sense that society itself was fragmenting. David Jones wrote *In Parenthesis* under the influence of Eliot (p. 205); his work also seeks to capture the fragmentary nature of experience through the modernist style.

? QUESTION

Of the different styles used by poets in this selection, which seem to you to be most effective in conveying the experience of the war?

The four post-war poets mostly wrote in more traditional forms; although Vernon Scannell's 'The Great War' (p. 223) is freer in style than the four-**stanza** format of Larkin's 'MCMXIV' (p. 222), for example, he still uses **rhyme**, albeit in an irregular way rather than to a fixed pattern.

Language and Style

 QUESTION

What differences in tone of voice can you detect in the war poems Stallworthy selects? Who are the supposed speakers and hearers of poems such as Binyon's 'For the Fallen' and Blunden's 'Report on Experience'? How does this affect your reactions to these poems?

The categories outlined in the previous section might lead a reader to expect a broad division between on the one hand **rhetorical** styles in favour of war and praising the dead and on the other a kind of anti-rhetoric used by poets of protest. This is far too crude, of course. Poets such as Sassoon and Owen often resort to high rhetoric in their denunciations of the war, as seen in the rhetorical question that concludes Owen's 'Futility', whilst Sandburg's 'Grass' is apparently artless in its simple, direct statements. It is more helpful to see that each poet seeks to select the most appropriate language and style for his or her subject and to assess how effective this is. In the case of Sandburg, for example, his use of 'Shovel' in the second line of his poem (p. 168) is an indication of the callousness he ascribes to nature. Or is that callousness the fault of those who have created war? The list of five famous battles implies that we can hardly blame the grass for growing on these battlefields, as the casual question of the traveller 'two years, ten years' later confirms. The piles of dead have been forgotten already: 'What place is this?' (ll. 7–8).

One approach is to explore how the poets use certain common words and **images**. Brooke's invocation of 'Holiness', 'Honour' and 'Nobleness' in 'The Dead' p. 162, ll. 10–14) and the **chivalry** of Herbert Asquith find few echoes in later poems. Brooke refers to 'sleeping' (in 'Peace', p. 162, l. 2); he claims that 'we' have been asleep until we find 'release' in war (l. 9). It is instructive to compare this with the way Owen concludes his conversation between dead soldiers in 'Strange Meeting' (p. 193): 'Let us sleep now ...'. For these men, it is sleep – the sleep of death – that is release. Hardy claimed in September 1914 that 'victory crowns the just' ('Men Who March Away', p. 160, l. 28). Sassoon in 'They' (p. 176) makes **ironic** use of the same word when he puts it in the mouth of his foolish Bishop: 'they'll have fought / In a just cause' (ll. 2–3). The rest of the poem shows the men's reward: lost limbs, blindness, syphilis and likely death. Sassoon clearly would not say like Brooke in 'Peace': 'Now, God be thanked Who has matched us with His hour' (p. 162, l. 1). Many poems imply sacrifice; two who use the word are Yeats and Blunden. Yeats, in 'Easter 1916' (p. 171, ll. 57–9), sees that sacrifice may not always be ennobling, perhaps qualifying his admiration of those who died in the Easter Rising:

> Too long a sacrifice
> Can make a stone of the heart.
> O when may it suffice?

Blunden, in 'Vlamertinghe: Passing the Château, July 1917', sees only too clearly that he and his colleagues are to be the victims and protests: 'But we are coming to the sacrifice' (p. 199, l. 2). Brooke praises 'the rich Dead' in 'The Dead' (p. 162, l.1) and has 'bugles blow' over them (l. 9); when the speaker in Cummings's 'next to of course god america i' mentions 'these heroic happy dead' (p. 202, l. 10) the reader is aware that this is merely empty rhetoric in the mouth of a demagogue. 'Lie' is a word frequently used by those rejecting the public justifications for the war. Owen calls the belief in patriotic glory 'the old Lie' in 'Dulce Et Decorum Est' (p. 188, l. 27); MacDiarmid denounces the 'lie' that the soldiers were anything other than 'professional murderers' in 'Another Epitaph on an Army of Mercenaries' (p. 168, ll. 1–3); whilst Sassoon's Officer has to resort to 'gallant lies' when describing the death of 'Jack' in 'The Hero' (p. 176, l. 8).

? QUESTION

How do the following poems make use of flowers: McCrae's 'In Flanders Fields', Thomas's 'The Cherry Trees' and Scannell's 'The Great War'?

For many writers as well as politicians and journalists, the war began with chivalry and ended in disillusionment born out of brutality. David Jones, although he seeks to convey the nobility of the common soldier, reflects this when, in the extract from *In Parenthesis* (p. 205, l. 1), he writes how 'sweet sister death has gone debauched today', in the one sentence conveying both the attractiveness of death to those still holding to the old codes and the sordid reality of modern warfare. There are more detailed discussions of language and style in the **Detailed summaries** and **Extended commentaries** to supplement this overview.

PART FOUR

CRITICAL PERSPECTIVES

 CHECK THE BOOK

Harold Munro, editor of the magazine *Poetry and Drama*, had a low opinion of the early war poetry, writing in September 1914: 'We get an impression of verse-writers excitedly gathering to *do something* for their flag, and as soon as they begin to rack their brains how that something may be done in verse, a hundred old phrases for patriotic moments float in their minds, which they reel into verse or fit into sonnets' (quoted in Samuel Hynes, *A War Imagined* (1992), p. 29).

READING CRITICALLY

This section provides a range of critical viewpoints and perspectives on the poetry of the First World War and gives a broad overview of key debates, interpretations and theories proposed since the poems were published. It is important to bear in mind the variety of interpretations and responses these texts have produced, many of them shaped by the critics' own backgrounds and historical contexts.

No single view of the poems should be seen as dominant – it is important that you arrive at your own judgements by questioning the perspectives described, and by developing your own critical insights. Objective analysis is a skill achieved through coupling close reading with an informed understanding of the key ideas, related texts and background information relevant to the text. These elements are all crucial in enabling you to assess the interpretations of other readers and even to view works of criticism as texts in themselves. The ability to read critically will serve you well both in your study of the text, and in any critical writing, presentation or further work you undertake.

ORIGINAL RECEPTION

Catherine Reilly's survey of poetry written during the First World War (see **Reading the Poetry of the First World War**), lists over 2,000 writers whose work was published in book, pamphlet or broadsheet form. Poems by established writers such as Sir Henry Newbolt appeared in *The Times* from the outbreak of hostilities, often among the leading articles, and up to 100 poems a day were sent to the newspaper in the early months of the war. Most of these were in support of the war effort, like Hardy's 'Men Who March Away', which was published in *The Times* on 5 September 1914, and Binyon's 'For the Fallen' which appeared on 21 September. This outpouring of poetry is an indication of a greater public appetite for poetry in 1914 than today – or at least for a certain kind of poetry. The anonymous editor of the very first war anthology, *Songs and Sonnets for England in War Time* (1914), wrote:

> In the stress of a nation's peril the poet at last comes into his own again, and with clarion call he rouses the sleeping soul of the empire. Prophet he is, champion and consoler.

Clearly these men and women felt that writing poems answered a need, either in themselves or their readers. It is also clear that most of this work has not survived as 'literature' – nor, we might guess, would many of the writers have expected the verse they contributed to newspapers or privately printed commemorative volumes to have a lasting appeal. After the initial outpouring of words, much of the writing about the First World War lapsed into obscurity, including work by poets whose reputations have been later revived.

Some poetry, however, achieved an immediate popularity that lasted beyond the war. Sorley's *Marlborough and Other Poems*, published in 1916 (he died in 1915), had run into six editions by the end of the year. By far the most popular 'war poet' was Rupert Brooke, even though his battle experience was limited to a day during the evacuation of Antwerp (he died from an infection on the way to the battle for Gallipoli in Turkey) and only his '1914' **sonnets** had anything to do with the war. Brooke was already an established poet when war was declared and his sonnet 'The Soldier' had been read from the pulpit of St Paul's Cathedral on Easter Sunday 1915 before appearing in *The Times*; Winston Churchill wrote his obituary for that paper. *1914 and Other Poems*, first published in 1915, had reached its twenty-eighth impression by 1920 and went on selling, whilst his *Collected Poems* of 1918 went through sixteen impressions in the next ten years. *The Muse in Arms*, 'a collection of war poems, for the most part written in the field of action, by seamen, soldiers, and flying men who are serving, or have served, in the Great War', first published in 1917, had been reprinted four times by 1919; as well as Brooke, Sorley, Sassoon and many lesser-known poets featured in that collection.

www. **CHECK THE NET**
The complete text of the 1917 anthology *The Muse in Arms* can be found on the First World War website, **www. firstworldwar. com**. Find it in the 'Prose & Poetry' section.

The work of men such as Sassoon and Owen, now regarded as the archetypal war poets, was less popular in its day. Although Sassoon's poems had been published in magazines during the war, his collection *Counter Attack*, published in the same month in 1918 as Brooke's *Collected Poems*, found reviewers less enthusiastic for his **realistic** approach and anger. The magazine *New Age* wrote:

> Mr. Sassoon rules himself out from the realm of poetry on two grounds: first he is quite indifferent to the creation of beauty; and second, he is prey to the emotions which tend to satire.

At the time of his death, Wilfred Owen had had only four poems published. Thanks to the advocacy of Sassoon and writers such as Edith Sitwell, his reputation began to grow and more of his work appeared in print, culminating in a collection of twenty-three of his poems called simply *Poems* in 1920, with an introduction by Sassoon. However, by 1929 the publishers had printed only 1,430 copies, with some still unsold, whilst Brooke's *Collected Poems* had sold 300,000 in the same period.

CHECK THE BOOK

The facts and figures regarding the sales of Owen's and Brooke's collections can be found in Samuel Hynes, *A War Imagined* (1992), p. 300 onwards.

If this sample of evidence from book sales demonstrates the varying fortunes of poets who feature in *The Oxford Book of War Poetry*, their own responses point up further differences. Discussions of poems in **Part Two** have shown how poets such as Sorley reacted against Brooke's words in 'The Dead' (p. 162) by writing in 'When you see millions of the mouthless dead', 'Say not soft things as other men have said' (p. 167, l. 3). Owen reacted against the jingoism of Jessie Pope and others, which he calls 'The old Lie', in 'Dulce Et Decorum Est' (p. 188, l. 27); and Pound, writing in 1920, savagely attacked in *Hugh Selwyn Mauberley* the 'old men's lies' (p. 210, l. 14) that had led 'a myriad' (l. 28) to their deaths. One interesting case is the poet and novelist Rose Macaulay. At the beginning of the war she had written 'Many Sisters to Many Brothers' which appeared in the popular anthology for 'boys and girls' called *Poems of Today* in 1915 (this volume was reprinted each year until at least the middle of the Second World War). The poem laments the lot of the sister condemned to sit at home whilst her brother is 'in a trench':

Oh, it's you that have the luck, out there in blood and muck:
You were born beneath a kindly star; ...
But for me ... a war is poor fun.

By 1916, she would seem to have regretted such sentiments, for in her novel *Non-combatants* she has a character write, in an essay on the 'Effects of the War':

War's an insanity ... This war's produced a little fine poetry, among a sea of tosh – a thing here and there; but mostly – oh, good Lord! The flood of cheap heroics and commonplace patriotic claptrap – it's swept slobbering all over us; there seems no stemming it. (quoted in Hynes, *A War Imagined* (1992), pp. 129–30)

LATER CRITICISM

Ezra Pound's indictment of the war in 1920 was an early manifestation of the attitude that was to become commonplace around ten years after the Armistice. In *Hugh Selwyn Mauberley*, Pound, who had observed the war from London as an American non-combatant, summarised in a few caustic lines what he saw as the betrayal of the generation of young men who:

... walked eye-deep in hell
believing in old men's lies, then unbelieving
came home, home to a lie,
home to many deceits,
home to old lies and new infamy; (p. 210, ll. 13–17)

Samuel Hynes summarises what he calls 'The Myth of the War', which became established with the publication of works such as Blunden's *Undertones of War* (1928), Remarque's *All Quiet on the Western Front* (1929) and Graves's *Goodbye to All That* (1929) and the production of Sherriff's *Journey's End* at the end of 1928, in these terms:

We know them all by now: the idealism betrayed; the early high-mindedness that turned in mid-war to bitterness and cynicism; the growing feeling among soldiers of alienation from the people at home for whom they were fighting; the rising resentment of

CHECK THE BOOK

The characters in R. C. Sherriff's play *Journey's End* (set in a dugout in 1918 and first performed in 1928) embody many of the stereotypes: Captain Stanhope, although commanding the company, 'is no more than a boy', having left his public school (where he 'was skipper of rugger, and kept wicket') for the army. Young Raleigh, straight from the same school, hero-worships Stanhope; he is assigned to the care of an older officer, Osborne (a schoolmaster who once played rugby for England).

profiteers and ignorant, patriotic, women; the growing sympathy for the men on the other side, betrayed in the same ways and suffering the same hardships; the emerging sense of the war as a machine and of all the soldiers as its victims; the bitter conviction that the men in the trenches fought for no cause, in a war that could not be stopped. (*A War Imagined* (1992), p. 439)

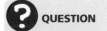

QUESTION

How do the poets in the Stallworthy selection reflect the 'myth of war'? Compare *Hugh Selwyn Mauberley* with Sassoon's, 'The General'.

The poetry of the First World War had, according to the accepted view, been very largely written during or very shortly after the conflict by those who took part. Whilst, as noted above, some volumes continued to be sold and presumably read, the establishment of the canon of 'war poets' was a longer process that began towards the end of the 1920s. It was as though writers of all kinds of literature needed a period of reflection and recovery before they could assess and react to what they had experienced – that, at least, would seem to explain why the classic war memoirs and fiction, along with the most popular 'war play', *Journey's End*, emerged at around the same time. For poetry, an important milestone was the publication in 1931 of *The Poems of Wilfred Owen*, edited by Edmund Blunden. Not only did it contain almost three times as many poems as Sassoon's earlier edition but Blunden also provided a long biographical memoir of Owen, quoting extensively from his letters home from the Front and the draft preface that Owen wrote, probably in May 1918, for a collection of war poems that he hoped to publish in 1919: 'This book is not about heroes. English poetry is not yet fit to speak of them.'

This preface (which Sassoon, too, had quoted) also established the phrase 'the Poetry is in the pity' as the touchstone by which 'true' war poetry was to be measured. So although, as May Wedderburn Cannan protested, not everyone 'came home with Siegfried Sassoon', the status of the 'soldier-poets' was established and along with it the category of 'war poetry' – which meant largely poetry of the First World War, and protest-poetry at that. There were exceptions: Isaac Rosenberg, for example, was less frequently mentioned than Owen, Sassoon, Blunden and Graves. Martin Stephen writes in his introduction to *Never Such Innocence* that as late as 1971 Rosenberg 'could still be described as the undiscovered genius of the First World War'.

There were influential figures who dissented from this view. Sir
Henry Newbolt, born in 1862 and author of pre-war patriotic verse
such as 'Vitaï Lampada' (p. 146), wrote of Owen's poems in a letter
in 1924:

> The best of them I know already – they are terribly good, but of
> course limited, almost all on one note … Owen and the rest of
> the broken men rail at the Old Men who sent the young to die:
> they have suffered cruelly, but in the nerves and not in the heart
> – they haven't the experience or the imagination to know the
> extreme human agony – 'Who giveth me to die for thee,
> Absalom my son, my son.' Paternity apart, what Englishman of
> fifty wouldn't far rather stop the shot himself than see the boys
> do it for him? I don't think these shell-shocked war poems will
> move our grandchildren greatly – there's nothing fundamental or
> final about them – at least they only put one figure into a very
> big equation, and that's not one of the unknown but one of the
> best-known quantities.

Another knight, Sir Arthur Quiller-Couch, was Professor of
English at Cambridge University and editor of *The Oxford Book of
English Verse*, first published in 1900 and often found in the kitbags
of officers at the front. When in 1939 (on the eve, that is, of another
war) he produced a new edition to include work written up to
'Armistice Day 1918', he found himself unable to approve of the
'fashion of morose disparagement; of sneering at things long by
catholic consent accounted beautiful; of scorning at "Man's
unconquerable mind" and hanging up (without benefit of laundry)
our common humanity as a rag on a clothes-line'. In consequence,
as might be expected of someone from an older tradition, the First
World War was represented by Brooke's 'The Soldier' (p. 163) and
'Into Battle', Binyon's 'For the Fallen' (p. 209) and one poem by
Owen, his 'Anthem for Doomed Youth' (p. 188)); Sorley, Sassoon
and Blunden were all included but theirs were not war poems. The
reaction of these older men against the brutal **realism** of Owen's
verse could have been predicted. W. B. Yeats, although of the same
generation (he was born in 1865), might have been expected to be
more sympathetic when he was invited to edit *The Oxford Book of
Modern Verse 1892–1935*. However, Yeats included few First World
War poems and nothing by Owen. In the preface, he wrote: 'I have

CONTEXT

Sir Arthur Quiller-
Couch's son, Bevil,
served in the First
World War only to
die in the Spanish
flu epidemic in
1919. Bevil was
engaged to the
poet May
Wedderburn
Cannan.

a distaste for certain poems written in the midst of the great war ... In poems that had for a time considerable fame, written in the first person, they made that suffering their own. I have rejected these poems for the same reason that made Arnold withdraw his *Empedocles on Etna* from circulation; passive suffering is not a theme for poetry.' When critics reacted angrily to this, Yeats wrote even more critically in a letter to Dorothy Wellesley in December 1936:

> When I excluded Wilfred Owen, whom I consider unworthy of the poets' corner of a country newspaper, I did not know ... that some body has put his worst and most famous poem in a glass-case in the British Museum ... if I had known it I would have excluded him just the same. He is all blood, dirt and sucked sugar stick (look at the selection in Faber's Anthology – he calls poets 'bards', a girl a 'maid', and talks about 'Titanic wars'). There is every excuse for him but none for those who like him.

CONTEXT

The poem Yeats refers to is Owen's 'Dulce Et Decorum Est'; it is still on public display at the British Library.

Yeats's rather intemperate reaction in this private letter may suggest more complex issues than just a disagreement about the nature of war poetry. Yeats was, after all, an Irish nationalist and had been a member of the Irish Senate; his reaction to the First World War at a time when Ireland was seeking independence from Britain can be gauged from 'On Being Asked for a War Poem' (p. 171): 'I think it better that in times like these / A poet's mouth be silent' (ll. 1–2). As his later poems in the collection reveal, Yeats was later greatly moved by the 1916 Easter Rising against British rule and showed his horror at the barbarity of the 'Black and Tans' after the war in 'Reprisals' (p. 175). It may also be, as Edna Longley suggests in *The Cambridge Companion to the Literature of the First World War* (2005), that Yeats was uneasy at the closeness of some of Owen's writing to the **images** in his own work – or that the genre of war poetry competed with his own as a model for young writers and led them astray, as he saw it, into more political, social-realistic poetry of the kind being written in response to the upheavals of the 1930s.

That period reached its climax when war broke out once more across Europe in 1939. This time there was no outpouring of poetry comparable to that of the First World War. The poet Keith Douglas (who died in action in 1944) gave one reason in his poem 'Desert

Flowers': that it had all been said already by the poets of the earlier conflict, 'Rosenberg, I only repeat what you were saying.'

CONTEMPORARY APPROACHES

In the immediate aftermath of the Second World War, as after the First, there was a period when it seemed best not to dwell on the horrors of war, though Dylan Thomas broadcast a spirited tribute to Wilfred Owen in 1946. Declaring that Owen may in future 'be regarded as one of the great poets of all wars', Thomas placed this evaluation in the context of the need to revisit war poetry in the era of the atomic bomb. He credited Owen as 'one of the four most profound influences upon the poets who came after him' – the others being Hopkins, Yeats and T. S. Eliot. This quartet is interesting in the light of the attempts by later critics to insist on a contrast between Owen and other war poets on the one hand and the **modernist** tradition, represented most notably by Eliot, on the other. Critical attention to poetry of the First World War was, however, limited during the next twenty years. One factor in the revival of interest came as an indirect consequence of the Second World War, when the new cathedral in Coventry was consecrated in 1962 to replace the medieval building which had been all but destroyed in 1940. Benjamin Britten (a lifelong pacifist who was born the year before the onset of the First World War) was commissioned to write a work for the occasion and chose in his *War Requiem* to combine the Latin Mass for the Dead with nine poems by Wilfred Owen, beginning with 'Anthem for Doomed Youth' and ending with a haunting setting of 'Strange Meeting'. This high-profile première by Britain's leading composer, using German as well as British soloists and at a time when there were demonstrations against nuclear weapons and the war in Vietnam, helped to create a fresh audience for Owen's work. Britten's recording of the work in 1963 sold 200,000 copies in the first five months alone, indicating unprecedented interest in a piece of contemporary classical music.

The establishment of what may be described as the modern canon of war poetry began with the appearance of a number of

CONTEXT

Britten remarked of his *War Requiem*: 'I hope it'll make people think a bit.' There are several recordings available, including one conducted by the composer (Decca Classics).

anthologies. The first of these was Brian Gardner's *Up the Line to Death* of 1964. 'A book written by the men who either witnessed or took part', it opens with Hardy's 'Channel Firing', written just before the war began, and ends with Philip Johnstone's 'High Wood' of 1918, describing an imagined tour of a battlefield by tourists after the war. This was followed a year later by *Men Who March Away*, edited by Ian Parsons. Like Gardner, Parsons arranged the poems thematically, in his case beginning with 'Visions of Glory' and ending with 'Aftermath'. The title is taken from Hardy's poem and Parsons concludes with Hardy's 'In Time of "The Breaking of Nations"' (both poems appear in *The Oxford Book of War Poetry*). These two anthologies became popular in schools; set as examination texts for 16- and 18-year-old students they defined an approach to war poetry which, whilst much wider than just a handful of poems by Owen and Sassoon, was described in this way by Gardner:

> After the Somme it was never the same again. The heroic days were gone. The disillusionment, already under way in the work of Siegfried Sassoon and Isaac Rosenberg, came out in an angry flood.

CHECK THE BOOK

See Lyn Macdonald's detailed study of the infamous battle, simply named *Somme* (1983).

Another influential anthology was *The Penguin Book of First World War Poetry* (1979). It was edited by the poet Jon Silkin who had already published a survey of First World War poetry called *Out of Battle* in 1972. In his lengthy introduction to this Penguin anthology, Silkin considered treatments of war by poets down the years before declaring his selection principles, which were 'that the poetry should have been to do with the war, and have been written by those who lived in, or through, the period'. His choices, he says, depend on 'excellence', 'apart', that is, 'from Brooke who appears as the representative of Georgian poetics ... and of that patriotism which distinguished the opening phases of the war'. Silkin's preferences can be seen in the selection of 'a great many poems by Rosenberg, and by Owen' as well as Thomas, Blunden and Sassoon. Silkin also reveals in his introduction that he believes that the true war poem is 'anti-war', though his argument is more subtle and developed than such a bald statement might suggest. A different line was taken by Catherine Reilly in *Scars Upon My Heart*, an anthology of 'Women's Poetry and Verse of the First World War' published in

1981. Reilly was determined that the women whose poetry she had researched in her 1978 bibliographic survey of First World War poetry should be heard. Judith Kazantzis writes in the preface:

> Is there among men, not excluding editors of war-poetry anthologies, the atavistic feeling that war is man's concern, as birth is women's; and that women quite simply cannot speak on the matter – an illogic which holds sway even when women have done so with knowledge and talent?

Reilly had revealed a bias, conscious or not, towards male poets: Gardner's anthology included no poems by women and Parsons admits to only 'one or two' by women (he actually included two). Jon Stallworthy, whose *Oxford Book of War Poetry* appeared in 1984, also includes only two poems by women in his First World War section. Silkin was moved to reconsider his selection when he produced a revised edition of *The Penguin Book of First World War Poetry* in 1996, including six more poems, all by women. Silkin wrote:

> Were these poems included under feminist pressures, or did you feel that these poems, because of their excellence, demanded inclusion? Having no simple answer, I feel I must say that feminism did require me to consider, again as scrupulously as I could, why, with the following exceptions, all the poets in the anthology are male ... A simple, perhaps too simple, reply is that the largest part of the suffering, and brutality, was borne, and inflicted, by men in this war.

Silkin goes on to admit: 'I had to expand my emotional register to include the tenderness as well as the outrage of grief.' Another neglected aspect of war poetry also revealed by Reilly was the large amount of popular or 'amateur' verse written at the time. This was given greater prominence, alongside the well established poets, in Martin Stephen's collection, *Never Such Innocence*, of 1988. Accompanied by extensive background information, Stephen presents a wider range than usual of work by the famous poets as well as popular songs and satires such as Major Owen Rutter's 'Song of Tiadatha' (the tale of an officer called 'Tired Arthur' in the much-parodied style of Longfellow's *Hiawatha*). The title is taken from Larkin's 'MCMXIV', with which the anthology concludes.

CHECK THE BOOK

For two feminist responses to the war from the 1920s and 1930s, see Virginia Woolf's *Jacob's Room* (1922), and Irene Rathbone's *We That Were Young* (1932). Woolf focuses on the constraints of living in a male-dominated society in the lead-up to the war, while Rathbone's is a strongly anti-war novel, told from the perspective of a former suffragette working as a nurse on the front line.

Publishers continue to produce anthologies of war poetry, so it seems there is still a demand. The Poet Laureate, Andrew Motion, edited *First World War Poems* for Faber in 2003, commenting in his introduction:

> Poetry of the First World War is still a part of the staple diet in our schools, which means it's still dripped into the national bloodstream at a steady rate. Its status as a sacred national text is confirmed every year on and around Armistice Day. And there is no reason to regret this … But there's a problem, all the same. The poems risk becoming less and less intimate as poems, as they are more and more widely accepted as state furniture.

In confirmation, if it were needed, of Motion's assertion that the war poets are now 'state furniture', in 1985 a memorial stone was unveiled in Poets' Corner of Westminster Abbey by the then Poet Laureate, Ted Hughes, commemorating poets of the First World War. Sixteen are mentioned by name: Richard Aldington, Laurence Binyon, Edmund Blunden, Rupert Brooke, Wilfrid Gibson, Robert Graves, Julian Grenfell, Ivor Gurney, David Jones, Robert Nichols, Wilfred Owen, Herbert Read, Isaac Rosenberg, Siegfried Sassoon, Charles Sorley and Edward Thomas. Around the names runs an inscription with Owen's words: 'My subject is War, and the pity of War. The Poetry is in the pity.' The critic Dominic Hibberd commented sceptically that there was no similar celebration of the work of the metaphysical poets or Victorian novelists, adding that he considered at least half the poets on the list to be distinctly second rate (though he did not say who those were).

At about the same time as the modern canon was being established critical works began to appear according a separate status to war poetry that had previously been given a passing mention or confined to considerations of the influence of individual poets such as Owen. The first was John Johnston's *English Poetry of the First World War* in 1964; this established the 'soldier-poets' as central but Johnston's proposition that only David Jones's *In Parenthesis* responded appropriately to the war by dealing with it in a **narrative** form has not found favour with subsequent critics. Johnston's value seems chiefly to lie in provoking reaction against what others considered his under-valuing of the poetry from the trenches.

QUESTION

Which three or four poems would you select to represent poetry of the First World War? What are the factors that determine your choices? Do you consider that there are aspects of First World War poetry that are not represented in Stallworthy's selection?

Bernard Bergonzi's *Heroes' Twilight* followed in 1965; although it deals with fiction and memoirs as well, poetry has pride of place. Bergonzi sees the First World War as marking the end of 'Hotspurian' heroism in literature and the advent of more anti-war views, which he characterises by identifying them with Shakespeare's 'fat knight', Falstaff. Heroic Hotspur perishes in *Henry IV* whilst Falstaff survives. A more explicitly anti-war stance is taken by Jon Silkin in his *Out of Battle* (1972). Confining himself to poetry, Silkin places the writers of the First World War in the context of the reactions of the nineteenth-century poets to radical politics. His readings of the poems are detailed and fair even when, as in the case of Kipling, he is unsympathetic to the poet's views; his chapters on Owen and, particularly, Rosenberg have proved influential on later critics.

The most influential work on literature of the First World War in the late twentieth century was undoubtedly Paul Fussell's *The Great War and Modern Memory*, first published in 1975. His claim that the war marked a profound shift in modern culture has set the agenda for subsequent critical discussion even for those who found his assertions exaggerated or simply wrong. Fussell broadened the focus from merely literary concerns – such aspects as the merits and impact of the war on English poetry – to explore what he considered to be the lasting cultural upheaval accelerated by, or even caused by, the war. Rather than deal with literature in isolation, Fussell considered the ways that the war reflected and altered cultural assumptions such as attitudes to nature, myth, literature and sexuality. By drawing together a wide range of material he demonstrated how many English writers responded in a 'literary' way to the war, in contrast to their American counterparts whose cultural background was different; his fifth chapter is called, evocatively, 'Oh What a Literary War'. For Fussell, the horrors of the war, although a product of nineteenth-century industrialisation, were so much worse than anyone had anticipated that they defined the outlook of culture for the rest of the century as **ironic** in attitude, fragmented and expecting the worst.

Subsequent criticism has invariably taken Fussell's analysis as a starting point. Modris Eksteins, in *Rites of Spring* (1989), takes an

CHECK THE BOOK

Writing of *The Oxford Book of War Poetry* in *Heroes' Twilight* (p. 212), Bergonzi says: 'It is difficult to avoid the impression that all the poetry which takes up the first half of Stallworthy's anthology is no more than an extended prelude to the war poetry of 1914–18.'

CHECK THE BOOK

In his 1996 appendix to *Heroes' Twilight*, called 'The Problem of War Poetry', Bergonzi writes: 'There is a danger when students, and indeed their teachers, take a handful of war poems, perhaps backed up by the spectacle of *Oh! What a Lovely War*, and treat them as sufficient evidence of what the First World War was all about' (p. 216).

even broader view, looking at the whole of modern culture, exploring, as the subtitle puts it, 'The Great War and the Birth of the Modern Age'. His starting point, as the title implies, is the famously controversial first performance of *The Rite of Spring* by Diaghilev's Ballets Russes in Paris in 1913. In the ballet, Stravinsky's music builds to a climax in which a young girl dances herself to death; Eksteins makes this the first act in an account of the excitement, horrors and aftermath of the war in European culture, in which **modernism** and the **avant-garde** came to dominate and which culminated in the destruction of Berlin by the Red Army in 1945. Samuel Hynes takes a similar approach in *A War Imagined* (1990). Hynes sees the creation of what he calls the 'Myth of the War' as a gradual process in the 1920s, resulting in the general acceptance of the view that the war destroyed nineteenth-century beliefs in progress and marked the end of agreement on cultural and moral absolutes. Like Fussell and Eksteins, Hynes sees the dominance of modernism in the middle of the twentieth century as being an inevitable consequence of the war, linking it to a central work by one of the leading figures of modernism, the poet T. S. Eliot's *Waste Land*: 'By the end of the Twenties, the War Myth and the Waste Land Myth were simply two versions of the same reality' (*A War Imagined* (Pimlico, 1992), p. 459). Jay Winter, in *Sites of Memory, Sites of Mourning* (1995), is less convinced; his survey of 'The Great War in European Cultural History' concentrates particularly on how the war was remembered, from official sites such as the Cenotaph in London's Whitehall to seances. He sees a continuation, at least in popular culture, of earlier traditions and ways of remembering the dead. It is a sign of the continuing interest in the literature of the First World War that Bergonzi, Silkin and Fussell have each produced revised editions of their works to take account of later critical responses.

PART FIVE

BACKGROUND

THE POETS OF THE FIRST WORLD WAR

The thirty-seven poets Jon Stallworthy includes in the First World War section of *The Oxford Book of War Poetry* came from a wide range of backgrounds. Because Stallworthy did not confine himself, as some editors have, to writers with first-hand experience of the war, some of the poets were not even born when the war ended – by which time eight were already dead. The oldest, Hardy, was already an old man of 74 in 1914; the youngest to serve in the war was Edgell Rickword, only 15 when the war broke out, and Edmund Blunden was only a little older at 17. Like many of their compatriots, these two young men went straight from school into the army; although they survived, many perished, including the promising young poet Charles Sorley, who died in 1915 at the age of 20.

The older poets were all well established at the outbreak of war. Kipling (1865–1936) was even more popular than Hardy and had been awarded the Nobel Prize for Literature in 1907, the first writer in English to receive the award. Kipling, who was born in India, had made his name with fiction such as *Kim*, *The Jungle Book* and *Just So Stories for Little Children* as well as a great deal of popular poetry. The Nobel Prize citation praised his 'power of observation, originality of imagination, virility of ideas and remarkable talent for narration'. Kipling, Hardy and Chesterton were amongst a group of writers called to a meeting in the first month of the war by C. F. G. Masterman of the Department of Information to encourage them to write 'public statements of the strength of the British case and principles in the war'. Others in the group included the poets Henry Newbolt and John Masefield and the novelists Arnold Bennett, H. G. Wells and Arthur Conan Doyle. Hardy seems to have gone straight home to write 'Men Who March Away' (p. 160). It might appear that even at this early stage, the contrast had been set up between 'the Old Men and the Young' (to borrow from the title of a poem Owen was to write later) – leading to the accusation

> **CONTEXT**
>
> Jon Stallworthy provides dates of birth and death of the poets in *The Oxford Book of War Poetry*, whilst the anthologies *Scars Upon My Heart*, *Up the Line to Death* and *Men Who March Away* have brief biographical notes on poets included. To find out more, see the sources in the **Further reading** section at the end of these Notes.

that, as Pound put it in *Hugh Selwyn Mauberley*, the young 'walked eye-deep in hell / believing in old men's lies' (p. 210, ll. 13–14). However, although each of these writers did contribute in some way to the war effort, they were not deaf to the effects of the war – Kipling, as mentioned in **The text: Detailed summaries**, was deeply affected by the loss of his son – and the work by both Kipling and Chesterton in *The Oxford Book of War Poetry* demonstrates a later awareness of the cost of the war. Hardy (1840–1928) had already written about the callous destruction of war in his verse drama *The Dynasts*. At least some of the younger poets admired Hardy's direct style and emphasis on an indifferent or even malign fate.

W. B. Yeats (1865–1939) was another member of the older generation and already regarded as one of the leading poets of the time – he was awarded the Nobel Prize for Literature in 1923. Despite this, as an Irish writer who had long supported the nationalist cause, he looked upon the war with an outsider's eye – at least (as recorded in **The text: Detailed summaries**) until events in Dublin in 1916, and the death of a friend's son, moved him to verse. Laurence Binyon (1869–1943) responded immediately by writing 'For the Fallen' in September 1914 (the fourth **stanza** is on many war memorials). Although too old to fight, in 1915 and 1916 he dedicated his annual leave from the British Museum, where he was an expert on Oriental prints, to working as a Red Cross orderly in France. Binyon understood, with anguish, at an early stage the devastation of the younger generation that was occurring. Binyon's poetry was of a traditional character, as can be heard in the **rhetoric** of 'For the Fallen', but he encouraged younger poets: Rosenberg sent him poems to consider in 1912 and Binyon wrote the introduction to Rosenberg's *Selected Poems* in 1922. He even came to admire the work of T. S. Eliot, despite the fact that when in 1919 Eliot gave a lecture on 'Modern Techniques in Poetry', chaired by Binyon, he described Binyon as 'a middle-aged poetic celebrity who evidently knew nothing about me except that I was supposed to be the latest rage, and he didn't understand it and didn't like it'.

Eliot (1888–1965) and Ezra Pound (1885–1972) did indeed represent the new world in more ways than one. As Americans, although both residing in Britain by 1914 (Eliot took British nationality in

1927), they challenged what they regarded as the stifling effects of the late nineteenth century on poetry. The **modernist** poetry which they wrote and championed became the dominant force after the First World War, leaving behind not only the older generation but also many of the 'Georgian' war poets (for more about this see **Literary background**). Eliot eventually became a leading member of the literary establishment. A Nobel Laureate in 1948, 'for his outstanding, pioneer contribution to present-day poetry', Eliot's criticism influenced university teaching well into the latter part of the twentieth century, and at the publishers Faber & Faber he encouraged many young writers. Other Americans in the First World War section of *The Oxford Book of War Poetry* include fellow modernists Robert Frost, John Peale Bishop, Carl Sandburg, Wallace Stevens and E. E. Cummings. Frost (1874–1963) also lived in England before the First World War, where he met Edward Thomas and encouraged him to turn his talents to poetry.

The archetypal 'war-poet' is perceived to be a young officer, educated at a public school and Oxford or Cambridge – possibly postponing his university place whilst he defends his county. Many of the 'young men' fit this stereotype but there are significant differences. Charles Sorley (1895–1915), whose father was Professor of Moral Philosophy at Cambridge, was educated at Marlborough College and left for a year's study in Germany before taking up his place at Oxford University. This was cut short by the outbreak of war and Sorely was briefly detained in Germany before returning to England and enlisting in the Suffolk Regiment. He was killed at Loos just over a year later. The same age as Sorely, Robert Graves (1895–1985) was also bound for Oxford when war broke out; he too had visited Germany and had relatives there (his middle name, which he tried to keep quiet as war approached, was von Ranke). In his memoir, *Goodbye to All That* (1929), he wonders whether his German cousins were in the trenches opposite his own. Graves volunteered as soon as war broke out – he claimed that this was in part to avoid another three years studying Greek and Latin. Seriously wounded, he was reported killed – but unlike Sorley, whom he greatly admired, Graves survived into old age and won considerable fame as poet, novelist and writer about mythology. Graves later suppressed most of the poems he wrote during the war;

 CHECK THE NET

Biographical information about a number of the poets in *The Oxford Book of War Poetry* can be found on the Poetry Archive site. Blunden, Eliot, Hughes, Larkin, MacDiarmid, Scannell, Sassoon and Yeats can be heard reading their own work here: **www. poetryarchive. org**

Siegfried Sassoon's time at Craiglockhart War Hospital in 1917 is the background to Pat Barker's novel *Regeneration* (1991) and Stephen MacDonald's play *Not About Heroes* (1982). Sassoon's lightly disguised memoirs, in which he appears as George Sherston, appeared as *Memoirs of a Fox-hunting Man* (1928), *Memoirs of an Infantry Officer* (1930) and *Sherston's Progress* (1936).

CONTEXT

Sassoon's protest against the war in July 1917 begins: 'I am making this statement as an act of wilful defiance of military authority, because I believe that the War is being deliberately prolonged by those who have the power to end it.' It appeared in *The Times* and was read out in the House of Commons.

of the three in *The Oxford Book of War Poetry*, two were written some twenty years later.

In the Royal Welch Fusiliers, Graves met and befriended Siegfried Sassoon (1886–1967). Sassoon had already spent time studying law, then history, at Cambridge but left without taking a degree. His wealthy family meant that he could pursue his own interests, which before the war included fox hunting, golf and writing poetry. His time in the trenches earned him the nickname 'Mad Jack' for his bravery, turned him into the angry, **satirical** poet represented in *The Oxford Book of War Poetry* and ultimately led him to protest at what he considered to be the unnecessary continuation of the war – and to throw the ribbon of his Military Cross into the River Mersey. Graves persuaded the army that Sassoon was suffering from shell-shock rather than refusing to serve and Sassoon allowed himself to be sent to Craiglockhart War Hospital. There a rather shy Wilfred Owen (1893–1918), also being treated for shock, asked Sassoon to sign some copies of his latest volume, *The Old Huntsman*. Owen sought Sassoon's advice on his own poetry; the manuscript of 'Anthem for Doomed Youth' now in the British Library shows alterations in Sassoon's hand. More importantly, Sassoon provided encouragement and contacts, so that Owen's first poems appeared in print.

One reason for Owen's shyness in Sassoon's presence was his less privileged background; educated not at a public school but at the local technical school in Shrewsbury, Owen had passed the entrance examination for the University of London but did not gain a scholarship and so could not afford to take the place. Instead he worked as a vicar's assistant before leaving to teach in France. Returning to England in 1915, Owen served in France. He and his men were trapped by a German bombardment in a flooded dug-out in No Man's Land for fifty hours. He suffered concussion when he fell down a well in the dark, then he was caught by a shell explosion which blew him into the air. He was diagnosed as suffering from neurasthenia (shell-shock), which is how he ended up in Craiglockhart War Hospital. There he edited *The Hydra*, the magazine produced by the patients, and, most significantly, met Sassoon and Graves. He carried photographs of the dead and wounded with him as evidence of the realities of the war for those who had only read newspaper reports. Returning to France, Owen won the Military Cross for bravery but was killed on 4 November 1918. The telegram reporting his death reached his parents as church bells were ringing to celebrate the Armistice on 11 November.

If Owen is now the best known of the war poets, Rupert Brooke was by far the most famous at the time. Born in 1887, he was a brilliant scholar and friendly with influential members of society, including the sons of Prime Minister H. H. Asquith. (Brooke sometimes stayed at 10 Downing Street when on leave and Arthur Asquith was one of the party that buried Brooke on the island of Skyros.) Brooke was a leading member of the Georgian group of poets; his first collection was published in 1911. Talented and good-looking, Brooke enlisted at once, was commissioned in the Royal Naval Division and saw limited action for a day during the evacuation of Antwerp before sailing to join the Gallipoli Campaign. On the way he contracted blood poisoning from a mosquito bite and died on 23 April 1915 (St George's Day). He became a national hero with the help of the Dean of St Paul's Cathedral, who read 'The Soldier' from his pulpit on Easter Day. Winston Churchill – at the time First Lord of the Admiralty, the Cabinet minister responsible for the Navy (he had organised Brooke's commission) – wrote in Brooke's obituary for *The Times*: 'he was all that one would wish England's noblest sons to be in the days when no sacrifice but the most precious is acceptable'. Although Brooke remained popular during and after the war, his 'war poetry' (actually just a few **sonnets**) was not based on battle experience but reflected the patriotic fervour of the autumn of 1914. Sassoon later wrote: 'People used to feel like this when they joined up in 1914 and 1915. No one feels it when they go out again.'

Officers, who had the advantages of education, money and connections, dominate the list of First World War poets. The voice of the private soldier is much less often heard; Stallworthy includes just three First World War privates. 'The army is the most detestable invention on this earth and no-one but a private in the army knows what it is like to be a slave,' wrote Isaac Rosenberg. Like Sassoon, Rosenberg was Jewish, but unlike the wealthy, well assimilated

CONTEXT

H. H. Asquith was Prime Minister from 1908 to 1916. The eldest of his five children, Raymond, was killed in the Battle of the Somme in 1916. Herbert, the second son, wrote 'The Volunteer' (p. 163 in *The Oxford Book of War Poetry*); his brother Arthur had a distinguished military career.

CONTEXT

Isaac Rosenberg wrote in 1915: 'I never joined the war for patriotic reasons. Nothing can justify war. I suppose we must all fight to get the trouble over ... I thought if I'd join there would be the separation allowance for my mother.' (This allowance was paid to a soldier's wife or, if he was unmarried, to his widowed mother if she depended on him.)

CHECK THE POEM

The modern Welsh poet Owen Sheers has also written about the fighting at Mametz Wood; his poem (published in *Skirrid Hill*, 2005) was inspired by the discovery, whilst he was making a film about David Jones and the writer Wyn Griffiths, of a grave holding twenty First World War soldiers, their arms linked together.

Sassoons, Isaac Rosenberg's family were poor immigrants from Russia living in the East End of London. He left school at 14 and worked in an engraver's workshop until his artistic talents allowed him to study at the Slade School of Art. When he enlisted in 1915, it was against the pacifist convictions of most of his family; it seems poverty played a part in his decision. His short stature meant he joined a 'Bantam' regiment where his absent-mindedness often got him into trouble and he was often bullied. He had little time to write but managed to produce, in periods of respite, his finest poetry, work that is now considered some of the most significant to emerge from the war. Just as he was beginning to win some recognition – an extract from his play *Moses* was included in a Georgian poetry anthology in 1917 – Rosenberg was killed while on night patrol on 1 April 1918.

David Jones (1895–1974) was another artist-poet and a private, though he seems to have enjoyed the company of his fellow-soldiers rather more than Rosenberg. Although born and brought up in London, where his father was a printer, his family was Welsh and, as with Rosenberg's Judaism, this heritage was important to him. *In Parenthesis* contains many references to Welsh history and myth as well as Arthurian and classical legends and to aspects of Roman Catholicism, to which he converted in 1921. Jones was born in the same year as Graves and Sorley and, like Graves and Sassoon, served in the Royal Welch Fusiliers and took part in the bitter fighting for Mametz Wood during the Battle of the Somme in 1916 (Graves was wounded in the same attack). During this engagement, one Welsh battalion of 676 men lost 400 killed or wounded in one day. After the war, Jones achieved success as an artist. He began *In Parenthesis* only in 1928; its **modernist** style appealed to T. S. Eliot, who wrote the introduction to the work when it was published in 1937.

The third private soldier in Stallworthy's selection was also accomplished in two branches of the arts: Ivor Gurney (1890–1937) showed early promise in music and studied at the Royal College of Music before the war. His home county of Gloucestershire was always dear to him; it features in his poetry and he joined its regiment in 1915. He experienced fighting at both the Somme and

Ypres; he was gassed and eventually suffered a breakdown, diagnosed as shell-shock (though he was probably already suffering from some kind of mental illness), in 1918. He returned to his music after the war, studying with the composer Vaughan Williams, but his fragile mental health gave way again in 1922 and he was confined to a mental hospital for the rest of his life, another casualty of the war.

Although his selection is dominated by English-speaking males, Stallworthy widens his scope to include two poems by women and two translated from French. Elizabeth Daryush (1887–1977) was the daughter of the Poet Laureate Robert Bridges; educated privately, she later disowned the poetry she had published up to 1921. After the war she married Ali Akbar Daryush and lived for several years in Persia, now Iran. May Wedderburn Cannan (1893–1973), as her poem 'Rouen' indicates, served in the Voluntary Aid Detachment at a hospital in France during the first part of the war, then joined MI5 to work in the Espionage Department in Paris, where her arrival coincided with a shell from the Germans' 'Big Bertha' cannon which blew up in the street beside her, killing a horse and wounding two men. She was engaged to Bevil Quiller-Couch, the son of the poet and Professor of English at Cambridge, Sir Arthur Quiller-Couch; Bevil survived the war but died in the Spanish influenza pandemic in 1919. After the war, despite her skills and experience, she found it difficult to get a job. She wrote in her autobiography, *Grey Ghosts and Voices*: 'The Census for 1921 had found out there was in the country a surplus of women who, inconsiderately, had not died in the war, and now there was an outcry and someone christened them "The Surplus Two Million". *The Times* suggested that they might seek work abroad; the unemployment figures were swollen with these unnecessary and unwanted persons.'

The French poet Guillaume Apollinaire (1880–1918) was another victim of Spanish influenza, having survived a head wound, trepanning and military medicine. Credited with inventing the term **surrealism** and helping to define the artistic movement cubism, Apollinaire had Polish and Italian parentage but settled in Paris. There he became one of the leading **avant-garde** poets and friend of controversial figures such as the artists Picasso, Duchamp and

CHECK THE BOOK

For a variety of other texts in translation, see Ernst Jünger (German), *Storm of Steel* (1920); Jaroslav Hašek (Czech), *The Good Soldier Švejk* (1923); and Marc Dugain (French), *The Officer's Ward* (1998). Bernard Bergonzi suggests that in *Storm of Steel* 'it is as though the subject matter of Owen and Sassoon had been combined with the sentiments of Brooke and Grenfell' (*Heroes' Twilight*, p. 158).

CHECK THE BOOK

There is an appropriately surreal account by the poet Cendrars of the burial of Apollinaire on 13 November 1918 in the first chapter of Jay Winters's *Sites of Memory, Sites of Mourning* (Cambridge, 1995), together with a reproduction of a sketch of the poet in uniform by Picasso.

Braque, the poet, dramatist and designer Cocteau and the composer Satie. Although in many ways a rebel (he had been arrested, wrongly, when the Mona Lisa was stolen from the Louvre in 1911), he volunteered to defend his adopted country as soon as war broke out. Benjamin Péret (1899–1959), another French surrealist, also served throughout the war, fought again in the Spanish Civil War and then had to flee Paris for Mexico when the Germans invaded France in the Second World War.

Four poets in the First World War section of *The Oxford Book of War Poetry* were born after the war. War is nevertheless a significant theme in the works of both Ted Hughes (1930–98) and Vernon Scannell (1922–2007). Hughes's father was one of only seventeen in his regiment who survived Gallipoli; he had told his son occasional stories about the war when Ted was young but became increasingly silent as he grew older. Scannell's father also fought in the First World War; Vernon Scannell had first-hand experience of the Second World War and took part in the Normandy landings. He also deserted twice, his pugnacious character doubtless contributing to his success as a boxer for a while after the war. Scannell received a special award from the Wilfred Owen Association in recognition of his contribution to war poetry. Philip Larkin's contribution to war poetry is just one poem, the much anthologised 'MCMXIV', a phrase from which Martin Stephen used as the title for his anthology *Never Such Innocence* (Everyman, 1988). The final poet in the First World War section is Douglas Dunn who although born and now living in Scotland, studied at Hull University and worked for a while in the University library under Philip Larkin. Born in 1942, he says in 'War Blinded' (p. 225) 'that war's too old for me to understand', yet the sight of two old soldiers, 'one blind, one in a wheelchair', still moves him.

LITERARY BACKGROUND

VICTORIAN AND EDWARDIAN POETS

The writers with first-hand experience of the First World War were all born in the nineteenth century. In Britain, the late Victorian period was still dominated by long-established poets such as the

Poet Laureate Tennyson, who died in 1892. His response to the disastrous Charge of the Light Brigade in 1854 can be read on page 115 of *The Oxford Book of War Poetry*. Its celebration of heroism and **chivalry** in the face of almost certain death finds an echo in Sir Henry Newbolt's 'Vitaï Lampada' (p. 146), which reflects the expansion of the British Empire to cover a quarter of the world's population by the end of the century. Works such as these would have been found in the school books studied by the young men who joined the armed forces in 1914. More experimental verse was written by younger poets towards the end of the century, some of whom were influenced by French **symbolism** – writers such as Swinburne, Oscar Wilde and W. B. Yeats. Thomas Hardy, who by 1896 had stopped writing novels after the hostile reception given to *Jude the Obscure*, showed in his poetry the same kind of interest in rural life and the *Satires of Circumstance* (to use the title of his collection of 1914) that had featured in his novels. His work shows an awareness of the harsh lot of the rural worker (and soldier in poems like 'Drummer Hodge', p. 149, and 'The Man He Killed', p. 150) that is often missing from the more aesthetic concerns of his contemporaries. Yeats had shown in his early work the influence of the lush late-**Romantic** style of the 1890s, but already his interest in Irish culture and politics was taking him on a separate path. During the Edwardian period (1901–10) poetry was dominated by figures such as Walter de la Mare, John Masefield and Rudyard Kipling, whose work was very popular at the time but who now read like nineteenth-century figures.

THE TWENTIETH CENTURY: GEORGIANS AND MODERNISTS

There was a conscious effort by younger poets such as Rupert Brooke to find a new, more accessible style for the twentieth century. They found a voice in the *Georgian Poetry* anthologies edited by Edward Marsh from 1912, which took their name from the new king, George V, who had come to the throne in 1910 (and should not be confused with the Georgian period in British history, which covers the reigns of the first four Georges, 1714–1830). Although, like the Edwardians, the Georgian poets have been overshadowed first by the events of the First World War and then by the dominance of **modernism** in the years that followed, their

CHECK THE BOOK
The Parade's End novels by Ford Maddox Ford, published between 1924 and 1928, document the challenge to Edwardian values brought about by the Great War. See also W. Somerset Maugham's play, *For Services Rendered* (1932), which describes the effect of the war on the provincial middle classes. Sydney, blinded in the trenches, declares: 'I know that we were the dupes of the incompetent fools who ruled the nations.'

anthologies were extremely popular and provided a readership not only for Brooke but also for Sassoon, Graves, Rosenberg and Blunden. Owen, though he was never published in *Georgian Poets*, was proud to have won their favour, writing home to his mother: 'I am held peer by the Georgians.' Brooke, whose handful of **sonnets** in response to the outbreak of war made him seem a fixture in the literary establishment (at least until well after the war was over), achieved some notoriety for his attempts at graphic reality, such as his description of seasickness on a cross-Channel ferry. One of the Georgian poets' significant concerns was the idea of England and 'Englishness', as is clear in a poem like Brooke's 'The Soldier' – another feature which distinguishes them from their American and European counterparts. The American Robert Frost, whose own poetry often deals with rural life on his own farm, did however join a group of these poets, including Brooke, Lascelles Abercrombie, Wilfred Gibson and Edward Thomas, in the remote Gloucestershire village of Dymock in the summer of 1914. Thomas is the Dymock poet who most successfully conveys this sense of the earthy reality of the English landscape, an aspect of the **pastoral** theme in English literature which deals in some form with the contrasts between the simple and complicated life. Paul Fussell, in the seventh chapter of *The Great War and Modern Memory*, describes this as a distinctively British response to the First World War, noting the numbers of poems about flowers and shepherds in poetry collections likely to be found in soldiers' kitbags such as *The Oxford Book of English Verse* and *The Spirit of Man*, edited by Robert Bridges. Edmund Blunden ends his memoir *Undertones of War* (1928), writing of his relief to be returning safely to England, by reminding his reader of the link between the pastoral theme and the Garden of Eden, where the Devil was a serpent: 'No destined anguish lifted its snaky head to poison a harmless young shepherd in a soldier's coat.'

To writers with a European perspective, British concerns in the pre-war period seemed parochial. In the arts, the **avant-garde** was to be found in cities such as Paris or Berlin rather than London. Towards the end of the nineteenth century, the plays of the Norwegian Ibsen and the Russian Chekhov had introduced a new kind of **realism** and a questioning of accepted values that were largely absent from plays

? QUESTION

Compare the ways that these poems can be considered examples of pastoral responses to the war: Blunden's 'Vlamertinghe: Passing the Château, July 1917' (p. 199), Thomas's 'The Cherry Trees' (p. 179) and Frost's 'Range-Finding' (p. 169).

written in English before the war. George Bernard Shaw (1856–1950) – an Irish writer who looked on British society with a mixture of **ironic** detachment and amused **satire** – played a large part in introducing the works of these major European playwrights to London audiences. Shaw subtitled his own play *Heartbreak House* (written before the war but not published until 1919 and first performed a year later): 'A Fantasia in the Russian Manner on English Themes'. He noted in a long preface added after the war that the people of 'cultured, leisured Europe before the war' were unable to address the problems that faced them, just like their Russian counterparts in Chekhov's works: 'the same nice people, the same utter futility'. He continued: 'There was a frivolous exultation in death for its own sake, which was at bottom an inability to realize that the deaths were real deaths and not stage ones.' In this they were not alone; although the Boer War in South Africa (1899–1902) and, even earlier, the American Civil War (1861–5) had demonstrated the devastating consequences of modern weapons, these conflicts had taken place far from Europe and their painful lessons had to be learnt again on the Western Front and in the Dardanelles. Thus in 1909 the Italian Marinetti published a *Futurist Manifesto* in Paris, the centre of the art world, which was a celebration of 'the love of danger' and 'the beauty of speed'. Most notoriously, Marinetti declared in his ninth proposition: 'We will glorify war – the world's only hygiene – militarism, patriotism, the destructive energy of freedom-bringers, beautiful ideas worthy dying for, and scorn for woman.'

This love of energy and rejection of tradition was also seen in the short-lived British movement known as Vorticism, which published its own manifesto in the magazine *Blast* which first appeared in June 1914. This declared: 'BLAST sport' and 'BLAST – years 1837–1900'. Like Futurism, its language was deliberately provocative, violent and militaristic: 'Mercenaries were always the best troops … Our Cause is NO-MAN'S.' Although Vorticism, like Futurism, primarily involved visual artists – its members included Wyndham Lewis and C. R. W. Nevinson who both became important war artists – it was a much wider movement, with the poet Ezra Pound playing a significant part; the second (and final) issue of *Blast* in 1915 carried work by Pound and T. S. Eliot. It

 CHECK THE BOOK

For responses to the American Civil War, see the extracts from Walt Whitman's *Drum-Taps* on pages 121ff. in *The Oxford Book of War Poetry*. Rosenberg was a great admirer of these poems, writing in 1917: '*Drum-Taps* stands unique as War Poetry in my mind. I have written a few war poems but when I think of *Drum-Taps* mine are absurd.'

CHECK THE NET

You can view works by Wyndham Lewis, C. R. W. Nevinson and other war artists such as the Nash brothers on the Imperial War Museum website. Go to **www.iwm.org.uk**, select 'IWM Collections' and search the art database. The entry on Nevinson's 'Paths of Glory' explains how the work was censored for showing the dead and how Nevinson incurred further official displeasure by displaying the painting with 'Censored' across the front.

QUESTION

Richard Aldington was another important Imagist poet. How does his poem 'Battlefield' (p. 200) illustrate the principles of Imagism? Which other First World War poems would you compare or contrast with Aldington's?

indicates the determination of the forces of **modernism**, in all the arts, to make a break with the past – it is perhaps significant that the leading modernist writers in English were both Americans, brought up outside the British class and education system. Pound had already gathered a group of poets called the **Imagists** whose principles were explained in their magazine *Poetry* in 1913. Imagism marks a break with earlier poetry, including that of the Georgians, with an emphasis on simple, direct language free from **rhetoric** and the restrictions of regular **rhyme** and **rhythm**. Through the work of Pound and particularly Eliot, modernism was to become the dominant force in poetry after the war, when Eliot's *The Waste Land* (1922) seemed more successfully to reflect the anxieties of the times. Before the war, however, there was some overlap between the groups; D. H. Lawrence had poems in both Imagist and Georgian publications and Rosenberg's work shows the influence of both groups.

Poets, when they could find time to write, were at least able to have some of their work published during the war itself. As mentioned in **Critical perspectives: Original reception**, newspapers and periodicals regularly printed poetry, and works by writers such as Rupert Brooke were extremely popular both during and after the war. More **realistic** and experimental verse did not find such a ready market, although literary weeklies such as *The Nation* would publish work by writers like Sassoon, who also arranged for Owen's work to appear there. Some idea of the range of work that was printed at the time can be seen in the anthology *The Muse in Arms*, 'a collection of war poems, for the most part written in the field of action, by seamen, soldiers, and flying men who are serving, or have served, in the Great War', edited by E. B. Osborne and published in 1917. Section headings included 'The Mother Land', 'The Christian Soldier' and 'Chivalry of Sport', which sounds as though the collection represented the old, pre-war heroic views. However, although Brooke's 'The Soldier' and Grenfell's 'Into Battle' feature in the collection, there was also more realistic verse by Sassoon and Graves. Once the war was over, those who had survived found that, with a few exceptions such as Brooke, there was only a small audience for war poetry. The rising importance of modernism, shown in the growing influence of writers like Eliot and Pound who had remained in London throughout the war, meant that the surviving Georgian poets, such as Sassoon, were increasingly sidelined. Unlike Sassoon, Graves put the war behind him and, once he had completed *Goodbye to All That* in 1929, he left Britain and refused to allow most of the poetry he had written during the war to be published. Bernard Bergonzi expresses this divergence of critical approaches to war poetry in an appendix to *Heroes' Twilight* (1996) called 'The Problem of War Poetry':

> Owen and Sassoon are read as witnesses to a great national tragedy, and poets of direct human impact, despite their traditional form; while Eliot and Pound are read as the modernist writers who remade twentieth Century poetry.

Not all poets shared this view; Larkin and a number of others writing after the Second World War looked back to poets such as Hardy and Edward Thomas and shared their affection for the English countryside, whilst others continue to find the First World War a rich source of inspiration. Rosenberg's admiration for Walt Whitman's American Civil War poems has already been noted; one of the leading poets of the Second World War, Keith Douglas (1920–44) recorded his debt to the poets of the First World War in 'Desert Flowers' in 1943 when he wrote: 'Rosenberg I only repeat what you were saying'. The 'Great War' was not 'the War to End Wars' that some hoped it would be.

PROSE AND DRAMA

For writers of the older generation, these fragmentary groups embodied the threats faced by society at the beginning of the new century. Novelists in particular gave voice to anxieties about the *Condition of England*, as C. F. G. Masterman had entitled his study of Edwardian society in 1909. Masterman had seen a greedy upper class exploiting a discontented working class, with the middle class in between, empty-headed and lacking in values. In E. M. Forster's *Howards End* (1910), the house after which the novel is named represents the stability and continuity of English life which is threatened by the conflict between the values of business and of imagination and the arts. In *England After the War*, Masterman looked back on his earlier work from 1922: 'The world of which I then wrote had vanished in the greatest secular catastrophe which

CHECK THE BOOK
The comments by a reviewer of T. S. Eliot's 'The Love Song of J. Alfred Prufrock' in 1916 demonstrate the contrast between pre-war attitudes to poetry and those of modernist poets such as Eliot and Pound. In 'trying to describe modern life', Eliot had, the reviewer believed, forgotten that what matters in poetry is beauty: 'However much you may have observed the world around you it is impossible to translate your observation into poetry without the spirit of beauty controlling the vision.'

PROSE AND DRAMA continued

CONTEXT

Whilst London audiences were enjoying seeing costumes, as *The Tatler* put it, 'suitable to the sultry climate of Old Bagdad [sic]' in *Chu-Chin-Chow* in 1917, British soldiers were involved in fighting to capture the real Baghdad.

CHECK THE BOOK

Bernard Bergonzi writes: 'Not till R. C. Sherriff's *Journey's End* of 1928 did the War come home to London audiences, and then only in terms of public-school sentimentalities and Boy's Own Paper heroism. *Journey's End* neither sought nor achieved any new expression or new style of sensibility to correspond with its newness of subject-matter' (*Sphere History of English Literature: The Twentieth Century*, 1970, pp. 320–1).

has tormented mankind since the fall of Rome.' D. H. Lawrence had already expressed concerns about the English landscape, the threats of industrialisation and relationships between men and women in novels such as *Sons and Lovers* (1913). He was more savage than Masterman in his judgement in his novel *Kangaroo* (1923), which included an autobiographical account of wartime England. 'From 1916 to 1919,' he wrote, 'a wave of criminal lust rose and possessed England, there was a reign of terror, under a set of indecent bullies like Bottomley of *John Bull* and other bottom-dog Members of the House of Commons.' (Horatio Bottomley was an MP whose patriotic journal *John Bull* was strongly opposed to any settlement with Germany other than unconditional surrender.)

During the war, writers in all forms of literature faced new challenges. For playwrights, the Defence of the Realm Act, introduced as soon as war broke out, added further difficulties on top of the existing licensing system operated by the Lord Chamberlain and the commercial pressures to meet audience expectations. Theatre managers decided that audiences wanted escapist entertainment and they seemed to be right. The musical *Chu-Chin-Chow* became the stage's longest running show with 2,235 performances at His Majesty's Theatre after opening in August 1916. Based on the story of Ali Baba and the forty thieves, it had over a dozen scene changes, fantastic sets, big dance routines and exotic costumes. Any criticism of the war, such as Shaw's *O'Flaherty VC*, could not be staged. In Miles Malleson's *Black 'Ell* a decorated war hero, Harold, is haunted by the enemies he has killed and relives the deaths with horror. Along with Malleson's other work, *'D' Company*, the play could not be staged; copies of the script were confiscated by the authorities shortly after they were published in 1916 and the play denounced by a Cabinet minister as 'a deliberate calumny of the British soldier'. The London theatre scene only began to deal in any realistic way with the war ten years later, when Sherriff's *Journey's End* was given a single semi-staged performance in December 1928 after being rejected by many theatre managements. Sherriff's account of events in a dugout during the German advance of 1918 went on to be a huge success, a sign that the public was at last ready to hear about the grim realities of the war. It was as though a period of private mourning after the war was necessary before, in a change of mood that was felt across Europe, the devastation could be faced in public.

Erich Remarque's *All Quiet on the Western Front* had become a publishing sensation in Germany in 1929; within the year it had been translated into about twenty languages and made into an Oscar-winning American film. Remarque wrote in his preface: 'I will try simply to tell of a generation of men who, even though they may have escaped its shells, were destroyed by the war.' This work, and others that appeared at the time, such as Blunden's memoir *Undertones of War* (1928), Sassoon's own lightly disguised *Memoirs of a Fox-hunting Man* (also published in 1928, followed in 1930 by *Memoirs of an Infantry Officer*), Graves's *Goodbye to All That* (1929) and Frederic Manning's *Her Privates We* (1930), in their different ways, reflected the post-war mood of disillusionment as well as a sense of loss. They also marked in prose a feature that had already emerged in poems by writers such as Sassoon: the adoption of a **satirical** approach as the best way to accommodate the nightmare experiences. They were joined by Vera Brittain's 1933 memoir from the point of view of a VAD nurse, *Testament of Youth*. Although the majority of the prose writing was, like the poetry, written by men who had fought, women's voices were being heard. One of the earliest novels to deal with the effects of the war was Rebecca West's *The Return of the Soldier* (1918). It deals with the difficulties faced by three women when a shell-shocked soldier returns from the front having forgotten everything except his youthful first love. The journalist Evadne Price was approached to write a British spoof of *All Quiet on the Western Front*, to be called *All Quaint on the Western Front* 'by Erica Remarks'. She was so appalled by the idea that she made contact with a VAD ambulance driver and based her novel *Not So Quiet* (1930), which she wrote using the pen-name Helen Zenna Smith, on the diary the young woman had kept at the time. Like Remarque's novel, *Not So Quiet* conveys the wreckage of war, the disillusionment of those taking part and their inability to communicate with civilians at home.

MODERN APPROACHES

The poetry of the First World War has continued to be used as a touchstone for those writing about or reflecting on modern

CHECK THE FILM
The 1930 black-and-white film version of *All Quiet on the Western Front*, directed by Lewis Milestone, is a more accurate representation of the book than the 1979 television film version. Both film and book were banned by the Nazis as 'pacifist Marxist propaganda'.

MODERN APPROACHES continued

CHECK THE NET

Charles Causley (1917–2003) was deeply affected by the death of his father from wounds sustained in the First World War as well as by his own service in the Second World War. You can find out more about him and hear him read on the Poetry Archive site, along with Michael Longley, Simon Armitage, Tony Harrison and Jo Shapcott: **www. poetryarchive. org**

CHECK THE BOOK

Sebastian Faulks appears to have based part of *Birdsong* (1993) on Owen's poem 'Strange Meeting'. Stephen Wraysford and his men detonate a huge mine under the German lines. Buried alive, he is saved by a German doctor whose brother they have killed.

conflicts, including the poets Charles Causley, Michael Longley, Glyn Maxwell, Simon Armitage, Tony Harrison and Jo Shapcott (the latter two have both written about the conflicts in Iraq, for example). Writers of fiction and drama also continue to be fascinated with the period. Writing well after the Second World War, authors reflect the contexts of their own times as well as drawing on historical research. Joan Littlewood's Theatre Workshop interpretation of the First World War through musical hall songs, *Oh! What a Lovely War* (1963), interspersed with short scenes demonstrating the callousness of the generals, whilst statistics of the slaughter are projected onto a screen at the back of the stage, is a product of the period of the Vietnam War and the Campaign for Nuclear Disarmament, a time when slaughter on a far more horrific scale than the First World War could be achieved by pressing a button in a nuclear submarine. Peter Whelan's play *The Accrington Pals* (1982) shows, by the effects on the women left behind, what happened when whole towns sent their men to the Front, to have them slaughtered on one day. Stephen MacDonald's *Not About Heroes* (1982) dramatises the meeting at Craiglockhart War Hospital between Owen and Sassoon.

Beginning with Susan Hill's *Strange Meeting* (1971), which describes the unlikely friendship forged between two young officers at the front, there has also been a steady stream of recent fiction about the First World War. Pat Barker's *Regeneration* trilogy, which begins with *Regeneration* (1991) and is followed by *The Eye in the Door* (1993) and *The Ghost Road* (1995), also uses Craiglockhart War Hospital as a setting, introducing historical characters such as Sassoon and in particular the army psychologist Rivers. Barker's approach is informed by both modern psychological theory (which was just emerging at the beginning of the twentieth century) and women's studies (which also see the First World War as a turning point in the role of women in British society). *Birdsong* (1993) by Sebastian Faulks is another novel that marks the resurgence of interest in the war at the end of the twentieth century; Faulks frames the wartime **narrative** with the quest in 1978 by the granddaughter of his First World War soldier for the story behind his silence after the war. Sebastian Barry adopts an Irish perspective in his 2005 novel, *A Long Long Way*, which explores the tensions created when a young Irish man, the son of a Dublin policeman, enlists to fight in France; his return home on leave only to be caught up in the Easter Rising of 1916 is in its way as traumatic for him as the fighting at the front.

HISTORICAL BACKGROUND

'The First World War was the great military and political event of its time; but it was also the great *imaginative* event', Samuel Hynes writes in the introduction to *A War Imagined: The First World War and English Culture* (1990). He explains the war's continuing fascination for subsequent generations: 'It altered the ways in which men and women thought not only about war but about the world, and about culture and its expressions.' The war also continues to be a subject of controversy for historians, even at this distance. For students of the literature of the First World War, a brief outline should suffice to indicate the shape of the war, which can be supplemented by the information given in the **Chronology**, in the materials mentioned in the **Further Reading** section and in **The text: Detailed summaries**.

The origins of the conflict which broke out in the summer of 1914 can be traced back to the preceding century. Following German unification in 1871 after the humiliating defeat of France in the Franco-Prussian War of 1870 and the loss of Alsace–Lorraine, German industrialisation and economic expansion proceeded at a rapid pace. By the end of the nineteenth century Germany was the leading Western nation for science, industry and scholarship and a powerful force in the arts. Both Sorely and Eliot went to study in Germany in 1914; Sassoon's mother was such an enthusiast for the operas of the German composer Wagner (1813–83) that she named her son Siegfried after the hero of the Ring Cycle. An arms race developed, in which Britain and Germany in particular sought to outclass each other's navy – for Britain, as an island nation, the Royal Navy was seen as the first line of defence. A large-scale army was not considered necessary and, unlike France and Germany, Britain relied on volunteers rather than conscription, supplemented by locally raised forces in the Empire (such as the 'Sepoy' mentioned by Kipling in his 'Epitaphs of the War').

 QUESTION

Why do you think the First World War has continued to attract writers many years afterwards? Can you detect any changing attitudes and approaches over the years?

CONTEXT

A succinct overview of the period can be found in *The Penguin Atlas of British and Irish History*. It has a four-page section on the Western Front and deals with other theatres of war, the Suffragettes, Ireland and other issues of the time.

CHECK THE NET
The BBC History site has a valuable section on the First World War, including an animated map of the Western Front and virtual tours of the trenches. See **www.bbc.co.uk/ history**

 CHECK THE BOOK
Alan Bleasdale's play, *The Monocled Mutineer* (1986), caused controversy when it was adapted for TV by the BBC. It tells the story of Percy Topliss who, according to the original book by William Allison and John Fairley's, led a mutiny of British soldiers before the Battle of Passchendaele. Whether in fact there was a mutiny has been debated by historians, soldiers and politicians.

The assassination of Archduke Franz Ferdinand of Austria–Hungary in Sarajevo on 28 June 1914 was the event that precipitated the war that engulfed Europe. Blaming Serbia for this murder, Austria–Hungary issued an ultimatum that led to war with Serbia on 28 July. Russia supported its Serbian ally and, in rapid succession at the beginning of August 1914, Germany declared war on Russia and France and, on 4 August, invaded neutral Belgium in order to bypass French defences and strike at Paris before Russian troops could mobilise. On the same day, Britain declared war on Germany citing its obligations to defend Belgian neutrality. In the capital cities of the major powers, the gathering crisis was followed by the public with rising anticipation and huge crowds thronged the streets, greeting the outbreak of war with excitement. The Germans made rapid advances; the small British Expeditionary Force was pushed back at the Battle of Mons and forced to retreat into France. Determined to defend Paris at all costs, the French and British forces drove the Germans back to the River Marne in September and both sides dug in to form the defensive positions that characterised the battlefields for much of the rest of the war. The front was extended until, by the end of the year, trenches stretched 760 km from neutral Switzerland to the Channel.

The war, at least on the Western Front that saw most of the casualties and features in most of the literature, became characterised by a series of set-piece battles that, unlike those of previous wars, sometimes lasted for months yet resulted in only small territorial gains. Ypres, a crucial barrier between German forces and the Channel ports, saw three such battles, in autumn 1914, in spring 1915 and, the largest and most costly, from July to November 1917 (also known as the Battle of Passchendaele). The longest battle of the war was at Verdun, from 21 February to 18 December 1916. Although there had been predictions that the war would be over by Christmas 1914, it soon became clear that the development of technology such as the machine gun and barbed wire gave the advantage to the defending forces. Air forces were primitive (although raids by Zeppelin balloons on London caused considerable panic) and tanks, though ultimately playing a part in the Allied successes, were only in their infancy. Another deadly technology was poisonous gas, first used by the Germans in 1915 and soon adopted by both sides – though it proved an unreliable weapon. The British achieved greater success with the huge mines they planted under the German lines; when nineteen of these exploded on 7 June 1917 the explosion was audible in Downing Street; 10,000 men were killed instantly and another 7,000 panicked and were captured.

Britain had at first relied on volunteers; Viscount Kitchener, the Secretary of State for War, called for an initial 100,000 men but 175,000 volunteered in the first week of September 1914 alone. By 1916, losses were such that Britain introduced conscription and with it, for the first time, the concept of the conscientious objector as someone whose convictions prevented him from bearing arms. During the 1916 Battle of the Somme there were horrific losses. On the first day alone (1 July), British forces suffered 57,470 casualties including 20,000 men killed – the highest ever losses in British military history. The war had become one of costly attrition, as each side pushed more and more men into battle, and the old notions of heroic warfare were buried in the mud.

The anticipated war at sea brought only one, inconclusive, battle at Jutland in 1916. This did, nevertheless, deny the German navy freedom at sea except by submarine warfare, which was used to attack Allied supplies from the Empire and the USA. Britain also sought to widen the scope of the war by launching a naval and land attack on Turkey at Gallipoli in 1915. This ill-conceived attempt to clear a supply path through the Dardanelles to Russia was ultimately defeated, at great cost to the British, Australian and New Zealand forces. Control of the seas was, however, to prove an important factor in weakening Germany by the end of the war; when the German army broke through the Allied lines in a desperate last push in March 1918 and made rapid advances into France, the momentum was lost as the German troops were distracted into looting whatever supplies they could find to supplement their meagre rations. The entry of the USA into the war in 1917 meant that the Allies were assured of the forces needed to defeat the Central Powers, despite the capitulation of Russia following the Revolution the same year. The German counter-offensive of 1918 failed and the Allies broke through the German

 CHECK THE BOOK
Edmund Blunden wrote about the first day of the Battle of the Somme: 'By the end of the day both sides had seen, in the sad scrawl of broken earth and murdered men, the answer to the question. No road. No thoroughfare. Neither race had won, nor could win, the War. The War had won, and would go on winning.'

 CHECK THE FILM
The official film *Battle of the Somme*, released in August 1916 whilst the battle was still raging, was intended to boost the war effort. It was seen by record audiences throughout Britain and abroad. You can see extracts from the film on the Imperial War Museum's special Somme site (see the section on 'The Opening Day'): **www.iwm.org.uk/ thesomme**

CHECK THE NET

The National Archives First World War site contains useful documentary materials on the war, from its origins to its aftermath. See **www. nationalarchives. gov.uk/pathways/ firstworldwar**

lines. Kaiser Wilhelm abdicated and the Armistice was declared on 11 November. The final shots of the war took place just metres away from the spot where the first engagement of British troops had taken place four years earlier.

The war left Europe exhausted and impoverished. The world-wide influenza epidemic which followed in 1918 claimed more lives, most of them young, than the war itself; its victims included the poet Apollinaire and the fiancé of the poet May Wedderburn Cannan. The Treaty of Versailles, which was signed in 1919, sought extensive war reparations from Germany and became a source of nationalist grievance in Germany over the next twenty years. Russia had been transformed into the Soviet Union under Lenin and was seen by the Western powers as a source of dangerous revolutionary ideas – there were Communist revolts in Berlin in 1919. Nine million men had died in the war, almost a million of them from Britain and its Empire. Although there were already more women than men in Britain before the war, that difference had swollen to almost two million by 1921. The gaiety of the 1920s hid the fact that a million women of child-bearing age were unlikely to marry and have children. It is not surprising, therefore, that as the storm-clouds gathered over Europe once again in the 1930s, the public did not greet the likelihood of war with the enthusiasm that had been seen in the capital cities of Europe in 1914.

World events	The poets' lives and works	Cultural events
1870 Franco-Prussian War (to 1871)		
1871 German unification	**1871** Thomas Hardy, *Desperate Remedies* (first novel)	
		1889 Henrik Ibsen's *A Doll's House* (play) in London
	1890 Rudyard Kipling, *Departmental Ditties, Barrack Room Ballads and Other Verses*	
		1893 Oscar Wilde, *A Woman of No Importance* (play)
	1894 Kipling, *Jungle Book* (novel)	**1894** George Bernard Shaw, *Arms and the Man* (play)
1895 Kiel Canal provides German navy with a fast connection between Baltic and North Sea		**1895** H. G. Wells, *The Time Machine* (novel)
1896 Marconi invents wireless telegraph	**1896** Hardy, *Jude the Obscure* (last novel); A. E. Houseman, *A Shropshire Lad*	
1899 Boer War (in South Africa, to 1902)		**1899** Edward Elgar, *Enigma Variations*
1900 British Labour Party founded		**1900** Arthur Quiller-Couch (ed.), *Oxford Book of English Verse*
1901 Death of Queen Victoria; accession of Edward VII; wireless communication between Europe and America	**1901** Kipling, *Kim* (novel)	
1903 Emmeline Pankhurst founds Women's Social and Political Union in Britain	**1903** Hardy, *The Dynasts I* (verse drama)	**1903** Robert Erskine Childers, *Riddle of the Sands* (novel)

World events	The poets' lives and works	Cultural events
1904 Russo-Japanese War (to 1905)		**1904** Anton Chekhov, *The Cherry Orchard* (play)
1906 Liberal Party wins British election; 30 Labour MPs; British *Dreadnought* battleship launched		**1906** John Galsworthy, *The Man of Property* (first novel of *The Forsyte Saga*)
1908 Asquith becomes Liberal prime minister (to 1916)		**1908** E. M. Forster, *A Room With a View* (novel)
1909 Bleriot flies across the English Channel	**1909** Hardy, *Time's Laughingstocks*	**1909** Filippo Marinetti, *Futurist Manifesto*
1910 Death of Edward VII; accession of George V		**1910** First Post-Impressionist exhibition in London; Forster, *Howards End* (novel)
1911 Railway and dock strikes in Britain; national health insurance introduced	**1911** Rupert Brooke, *Poems*	**1911** J. M. Barrie, *Peter Pan* (play); Joseph Conrad, *Under Western Eyes* (novel)
1912 Sinking of the *Titanic*; the Third Home Rule Bill proposes self-government for Ireland; Balkan War	**1912** *Georgian Poetry 1911–12* (first anthology, ed. Edward Marsh)	
1913 Second and Third Balkan Wars		**1913** Albert Einstein, *Theory of Relativity*; Igor Stravinsky, *Le Sacre du Printemps*; D. H. Lawrence, *Sons and Lovers* (novel)
1914 (20 March) Curragh mutiny; (28 June) assassination of Archduke Franz Ferdinand; (28 July) Austria–Hungary declares war on Serbia; (1–4 August) Germany declares war on Russia and France, German troops enter Belgium	**1914** Charles Sorley, Siegfried Sassoon, John McCrae, Robert Graves, Rupert Brooke enlist; Laurence Binyon, 'For the Fallen'; Ezra Pound, *Des Imagistes*; Hardy, *Satires of Circumstance*; Edmund Blunden, *Poems 1913 and 1914*; W. B. Yeats, *Responsibilities*	**1914** James Joyce, *Dubliners* (short stories); Wyndham Lewis founds *Blast* as journal of Vorticism

World events	The poets' lives and works	Cultural events
1914 cont (4 August) Britain declares war on Germany and President Wilson declares US neutrality; Battles of Mons and the Marne; first Battles of Aisne and Ypres; Turkey enters war on side of Central Powers; (December) unofficial Christmas truce on parts of Western Front		
1915 German U-boat attacks on Allied and neutral shipping; sinking of the *Lusitania* causes diplomatic crisis between Germany and USA; Dardanelles campaign; Gallipoli landings; first gas attack at second Battle of Ypres; (23 May) Italy declares war on Austria–Hungary; Battle of Loos (Britain uses gas for first time); (December) retreat from Gallipoli; Haig becomes Commander in Chief of British Expeditionary Force (BEF)	**1915** Ivor Gurney, Edward Thomas, David Jones, Blunden, Wilfred Owen, Isaac Rosenberg enlist; deaths of Brooke, Sorely, Julian Grenfell and Kipling's son; McCrae, 'In Flanders Fields'; Brooke, *1914 and Other Poems*; *Georgian Poetry 1913–15*	**1915** John Buchan, *The Thirty-nine Steps* (novel); Lawrence, *The Rainbow* (novel, banned in Britain); Edith Wharton, *Fighting France: From Dunkerque to Belfort* (collected articles)
1916 Conscription introduced in Britain; Battle of Verdun (longest battle of war, 400,000 casualties on each side); Easter Rising in Dublin; naval Battle of Jutland – Kitchener drowned; (1 July) Somme offensive begins (57,470 British casualties on first day including 20,000 killed; total casualties on both sides over one million); Lloyd George becomes prime minister	**1916** Richard Aldington conscripted; Graves reported dead; Blunden and Sassoon awarded Military Cross; Sorley, *Marlborough and Other Poems*; Robert Bridges (ed.), *The Spirit of Man* (poetry)	**1916** Henri Barbusse, *Le Feu* (novel); Buchan, *Greenmantle* (novel); Joyce, *A Portrait of the Artist as a Young Man* (novel); Wells, *Mr Britling Sees it Through* (novel); Miles Malleson *Black 'Ell* and '*D*' *Company* (plays, suppressed); film *Battle of the Somme* shown to record audiences throughout Britain and abroad

World events

1917 British forces take Baghdad; Russian revolutions – Tsar abdicates and Communist government under Lenin; USA declares war on Germany; Arras offensive; mutiny in French army; third Battle of Ypres (Passchendaele); British forces enter Jerusalem; Russia begin peace negotiations with Germany; Battle of Cambrai (first major tank battle)

1918 (3 March) Russian peace agreement with Germany; German spring offensive; Tsar and family murdered by Bolsheviks; German retreat at the Marne; German fleet mutinies; Kaiser abdicates; (11 November) Armistice; votes in Britain for women over 30, men over 21; world-wide influenza epidemic kills 20 million people

1919 Draft covenant for the League of Nations; (28 June) Treaty of Versailles; (19 July) victory march in London; (11 November) first two-minute silence on Armistice Day; first British woman MP

1920 First meeting of the League of Nations; civil war in Ireland; Home Rule Act; (11 November) unveiling of Lutyens's permanent Cenotaph in Whitehall

The poets' lives and works

1917 Deaths of T. E. Hulme, Thomas; Sassoon's statement against the war and he is sent to Craiglockhart; Sassoon meets Owen; Graves meets Owen; Thomas, *Poems*; Sassoon, *The Old Huntsman*; Graves, *Fairies and Fusiliers*; Gurney, *Severn and Somme*; Yeats, *The Wild Swans at Coole*; *Georgian Poetry 1916–17*; T. S. Eliot, *Prufrock and Other Observations*

1918 Owen awarded Military Cross; deaths of Owen, McCrae, Rosenberg, Guillaume Apollinaire; Sassoon, *Counter-Attack*; Thomas, *Last Poems*

1919 Eliot, *Poems*; Sassoon, *War Poems*; McCrae, *Flanders Fields and Other Poems*; Hardy, *Collected Poems*; *Georgian Poetry 1918–19*

1920 Owen, *Poems* (ed. Sassoon); Pound, *Hugh Selwyn Mauberley*; Eliot, *The Sacred Wood: Essays on Poetry and Criticism*

Cultural events

1917 Sigmund Freud, *Introduction to Psychoanalysis*; C. R. W. Nevinson, *Paths Of Glory* (painting censored by War Office when first exhibited in 1918); Gustav Holst, *The Planets: Suite for Large Orchestra*

1918 Rebecca West, *Return of the Soldier* (novel); Lytton Strachey, *Eminent Victorians* (history)

1919 John Maynard Keynes, *The Economic Consequences of the Peace*; Edward Elgar, *Cello concerto*; Paul Nash, *The Menin Road* (painting)

1920 Lawrence, *Women in Love* (novel); Ernst Jünger, *In Stahlgewittern* (novel); George Bernard Shaw, *Heartbreak House* (play)

World events

1921 Unemployment in Britain reaches post-war high of 2.5 million; partition of Ireland establishes Irish Free State; (11 November) first British Legion Poppy Day

1922 BBC established; Fascist revolution in Italy; Stalin becomes General Secretary of Russian Communist Party; Irish Civil War (to 1923)

1923 USSR established; collapse of German currency; French occupy the Ruhr

1924 Lenin dies, succeeded by Stalin

1926 General Strike in Britain

The poets' lives and works

1922 Births of Philip Larkin, Vernon Scannell; *Georgian Poetry 1920–22* (final anthology); Eliot, *The Waste Land*; E. E. Cummings, *The Enormous Room* (memoir); Hardy, *Late Lyrics and Earlier*; Housman, *Last Poems*

1926 Sassoon, *Satirical Poems*

Cultural events

1922 Joyce, *Ulysses* (novel); Virginia Woolf, *Jacob's Room* (novel); Vaughan Williams, *Third Symphony* ('Pastoral')

1923 Jaroslav Hašek, *The Good Soldier Švejk* (novel); Lawrence, *Kangaroo* (novel); Adolf Hitler, *Mine Kampf*; Sean O'Casey, *The Shadow of a Gunman* (play); John Foulds, *A World Requiem* performed at British Legion's Armistice Night (and until 1926)

1924 Ford Madox Ford, *Some Do Not* (first volume of *Parade's End* novels); Forster, *Passage to India* (novel); O'Casey, *Juno and the Paycock* (play)

1925 F. Scott Fitzgerald, *The Great Gatsby* (novel); Franz Kafka, *The Trial* (novel); Woolf, *Mrs Dalloway* (novel)

1926 T. E. Lawrence, *Seven Pillars of Wisdom* (autobiography)

World events

1927 Menin Gate war memorial opens at Ypres

1928 Women's Suffrage Act in Britain – women given same voting rights as men

1929 Wall Street Crash in USA ushers in the Depression; Trotsky expelled from Russia

1930 Mass unemployment; Nazis elected to German Reichstag

1933 Hitler becomes Chancellor of Germany; Reichstag fire; Japanese occupy north China

The poets' lives and works

1927 Graves, *Poems 1914–1926*

1928 Death of Hardy

1929 Blunden, *Undertones of War* (memoir); Sassoon, *Memoirs of a Fox-hunting Man* (memoir); Aldington, *Death of a Hero* (novel); Graves, *Goodbye to All That* (memoir)

1930 Birth of Ted Hughes; Blunden, *Poems 1914–30*; Eliot, *Ash Wednesday*; Sassoon, *Memoirs of an Infantry Officer* (memoir)

1931 *The Poems of Wilfred Owen* (ed. by Blunden)

Cultural events

1927 Woolf, *To the Lighthouse* (novel)

1928 Sherriff, *Journey's End* (private performance)

1929 Ernest Hemingway, *A Farewell to Arms* (novel); Jünger, *Storm of Steel* (novel, English translation); Lawrence, *Lady Chatterley's Lover* (novel); O'Casey, *The Silver Tassie* (play); Erich Remarque, *All Quiet on the Western Front* (novel); Sherriff, *Journey's End* (play)

1930 Hašek, *The Good Soldier Švejk* (novel; English translation); Frederic Manning, *Her Privates We* (memoir); film *All Quiet on the Western Front* wins Oscar; Henry Williamson, *The Patriot's Progress* (novel)

1931 Noel Coward, *Cavalcade* (play)

1932 Somerset Maugham, *For Services Rendered* (play); Irene Rathbone, *We That Were Young* (novel)

1933 Vera Brittain, *Testament of Youth* (memoir); George Orwell, *Down and Out in Paris and London* (autobiography)

World events

1934 Peace Pledge Union founded (Sassoon amongst sponsors)

1935 Italy invades Abyssinia

1936 George V dies, Edward VII abdicates, George VI crowned king in Britain; Spanish Civil War (to 1939); Mussolini and Hitler form Rome–Berlin Axis; Germany re-occupies the Rhineland

1937 German planes bomb Spanish city of Guernica

1938 Germany invades and annexes Austria; Chamberlain signs Munich Agreement with Hitler

1939 Germany invades Poland; outbreak of Second World War

The poets' lives and works

1934 Graves, *I, Claudius* (novel)

1935 Eliot, *Murder in the Cathedral* (verse drama)

1936 Deaths of G. K. Chesterton, Housman and Kipling; Carl Sandburg, *The People, Yes*; Sassoon, *Sherston's Progress* (memoir); Yeats (ed.), *Oxford Book of Modern Verse*

1937 Death of Gurney; David Jones, *In Parenthesis*; Rosenberg, *Collected Works*

1939 Deaths of Yeats, Frost; Eliot, *Old Possum's Book of Practical Cats*

Cultural events

1934 Evelyn Waugh, *A Handful of Dust* (novel)

1936 Charlie Chaplin, *Modern Times* (film)

1937 Pablo Picasso, *Guernica* (painting)

1939 John Steinbeck, *Grapes of Wrath* (novel); Joyce, *Finnegans Wake* (novel)

FIRST WORLD WAR POETRY

Marcus Clapham, ed., *The Wordsworth Book of First World War Poetry*, Wordsworth, 1995

Rita Dove, *American Smooth*, Norton, 2004
> An interesting response to the war by a modern American poet; the 'Not Welcome Here' section is a sequence of eight poems about a group of African-Americans who fought their way to the Rhine in 1918

Brian Gardner, ed., *Up the Line to Death*, Methuen, 1964
> '[P]oems by men who witnessed or took part' in the war, arranged thematically with an introduction and brief biographical notes

Robert Giddings, ed., *The War Poets*, Bloomsbury, 1988

Christopher Martin, ed., *War Poems*, Collins Educational, 1990

Andrew Motion, *First World War Poems*, Faber, 2003

Vivien Noakes, ed., *Voices of Silence: The Alternative Book of First World War Poetry*, Sutton, 2006
> Collected from contemporary newspapers and magazines, gift books and postcards

I. M. Parsons, ed., *Men Who March Away*, Chatto & Windus, 1965; Heinemann Education edition also available
> Poems arranged thematically, mostly by men who took part in the war, with an introduction and brief biographical notes

Catherine Reilly, ed., *Scars Upon My Heart: Women's Poetry and Verse of the First World War*, Virago, 1981
> Arranged alphabetically, with an introduction and brief biographies

Jon Silkin, ed., *The Penguin Book of First World War Poetry*, 1st edn 1979, considerably revised in 1981 and 1996
> Includes some poems in translation and a lengthy introduction

Martin Stephen, ed., *Never Such Innocence*, Buchan & Enright 1988; Everyman edition, 1991
> Very broad selection, with helpful introductions to each section

Work by most of the poets featured in *The Oxford Book of War Poetry* is available in collected and selected editions, for example:

Edmund Blunden, *Undertones of War*, Penguin, 2000
  Contains a useful 'Supplement of Poetical Interpretations and Variations'

Jon Stallworthy, *The War Poems of Wilfred Owen*, Chatto & Windus, 1995

LITERARY CRITICISM AND CULTURAL COMMENTARY

Andrew Barlow, *The Great War in British Literature*, Cambridge, 2000
  Succinct overview with brief anthology of poems and extracts from fiction and drama, together with assignments for students

Bernard Bergonzi, *Heroes' Twilight*, Constable, 1965; 3rd edn, Carcanet, 1996
  Comprehensive and valuable survey of poetry, fiction and autobiographical writing of the First World War; the revised edition covers modern writers and responds to recent criticism

Modris Eksteins, *Rites of Spring: The Great War and the Birth of the Modern Age*, Bantam, 1989
  Stimulating and wide-ranging account of how, in his view, the whole of modern culture was transformed by the war; ranges across Europe and across art forms

Paul Fussell, *The Great War and Modern Memory*, Oxford, 1975; 2000
  The most influential modern work on literature of the First World War, setting the agenda for subsequent critical discussion by exploring the lasting cultural upheaval caused by the war. The 2000 edition contains an afterword discussing responses to the 1st edition

Samuel Hynes, *A War Imagined: The First World War and English Culture*, Bodley Head, 1990; 1992
  Explores the creation of the 'Myth of the War' through a detailed and readable cultural history full of insights into the literature of the period; like Eksteins, Hynes sees the dominance of modernism as an inevitable consequence of the war

Vincent Sherry, ed., *The Cambridge Companion to the Literature of the First World War*, Cambridge, 2005
  Up-to-date critical overview of the literature of the war, including useful section on European and American literature and cinema

Jay Winter, *Sites of Memory, Sites of Mourning: The Great War in European Cultural History*, Cambridge, 1995
> Explores how the war was remembered; ranges widely to include examples from France and Germany, but emphasises the continuation of more traditional forms of mourning

The following volumes deal specifically with the poetry of the First World War:

John Greening, *Student Guide to Poets of the First World War*, Greenwich Exchange, 2004
> Succinct but informative chapters on ten poets, with additional material on other key poems and modern responses to the First World War and more recent conflicts; not afraid to challenge widely held views

Dominic Hibberd, ed., *Poetry of the First World War*, Casebook series, Macmillan, 1981
> Useful range of essays, especially the earlier material on reception up to 1946; inevitably does not take account of recent criticism

Dominic Hibberd, *Wilfred Owen: A New Biography*, Weidenfeld & Nicolson, 2002
> Detailed study in the light of new material

Jon Silkin, *Out of Battle: The Poetry of the Great War*, Oxford University Press, 1972; revised edn, Routledge Ark Paperback, 1987; also published by Palgrave Macmillan
> Detailed and sensitive readings of poets from Hardy to David Jones; Silkin was an early and convincing champion of Rosenberg

Jon Stallworthy, *Wilfred Owen: A Biography*, Oxford University Press, 1974
> Readable biography with sensitive responses to the poetry; includes facsimiles of a number of key poems

Jon Stallworthy, *Anthem for Doomed Youth: Twelve Soldier Poets of the First World War*, Constable, 2002
> Produced to accompany an exhibition at the Imperial War Museum, this lavishly illustrated large-format volume introduces selected poems from the twelve poets, with biographical and critical information

WIDER READING IN FIRST WORLD WAR LITERATURE

The dates for these texts indicate when they were first published or, in the case of plays and films, produced. For connections and comparisons between many of these texts and the poetry of the First World War see the relevant pages of these Notes (provided in bold below):

FICTION

Pat Barker, *Regeneration* trilogy – *Regeneration* (1990), *The Eye in the Door* (1993) and *The Ghost Road* (1995) **(pp. 122, 134)**

Sebastian Barry, *A Long Long Way* (2005) **(pp. 33, 50, 134)**

Ben Elton, *The First Casualty* (2005) **(p. 66)**

Sebastian Faulks, *Birdsong* (1993) **(p. 134)**

Ford Maddox Ford, *Parade's End* novels – *Some Do Not...* (1924), *No More Parades* (1925), *A Man Could Stand Up* (1926) and *The Last Post* (1928) **(p. 127)**

Ernest Hemingway, *A Farewell to Arms* (1929) **(p. 101)**

Susan Hill, *Strange Meeting* (1971) **(pp. 92, 134)**

Frederic Manning, *Her Privates We* (1930) **(pp. 83, 133)**

Irene Rathbone, *We That Were Young* (1932) **(p. 115)**

Helen Zenna Smith, *Not So Quiet* (1930) **(p. 133)**

Rebecca West, *Return of the Soldier* (1918) **(p. 133)**

Virginia Woolf, *Jacob's Room* (1922) **(p. 115)**

MEMOIRS

Edmund Blunden, *Undertones of War* (1928) **(pp. 61, 63, 109, 128, 133)**

Vera Brittain, *Testament of Youth* (1933) **(p. 133)**

Robert Graves, *Goodbye to All That* (1929) **(pp. 59–60, 109, 121, 133)**

Siegfried Sassoon, *Memoirs of an Infantry Officer* (1930) **(pp. 36, 122, 133)**

HISTORY AND TESTIMONY

William Allison and John Fairley, *The Monocled Mutineer* (1978)

Max Arthur, ed., *Forgotten Voices of the Great War* (2002)

Max Arthur, *Last Post* (2005)

Correlli Barnett, *The Great War* (1979), based on BBC Television series broadcast in 1964

Richard van Emden, *The Trench* (2002)

Richard Holmes, *Tommy* (2005)

Lyn Macdonald, *Somme* (1983)

Ben MacIntyre, *A Foreign Field* (2001)

DIARIES, LETTERS AND BIOGRAPHY

Alan Bishop, ed., *Chronicle of Youth: Vera Brittain's War Diary* (1981)

Alan Bishop and Mark Bostridge, eds, *Letters from a Lost Generation* (1998)

Bodleian Library of Oxford University, *A Month at the Front, Diary of an Unknown Soldier* (2006)

Svetlana Palmer and Sarah Wallis, eds, *A War in Words: The First World War in Diaries and Letters* (2003)

Michael Walsh, *Brothers in War* (2006)

COLLECTIONS

Agnes Cardinal, Dorothy Goldman and Judith Hattaway, eds, *Women's Writing on the First World War* (1999)

Joyce Marlow, ed., *The Virago Book of Women and the Great War* (1998)

DRAMA

Alan Bleasdale, *The Monocled Mutineer* (1986) **(p. 136)**

Richard Curtis and Ben Elton, *Blackadder Goes Forth* (1989) **(p. 8)**

Joan Littlewood, *Oh! What a Lovely War* (1963) **(p. 134)**

Stephen MacDonald, *Not About Heroes* (1982) **(p. 48, 122, 134)**

Miles Malleson, *Black 'Ell* (1916) **(p. 132)**

W. Somerset Maugham, *For Services Rendered* (1932) **(p. 127)**

Frank McGuinness, *Observe the Sons of Ulster Marching Towards the Somme* (1986) **(p. 33)**

Sean O'Casey, *The Silver Tassie* (1929) **(p. 32)**

George Bernard Shaw, *Heartbreak House* (1919) **(p. 129)**

George Bernard Shaw, *O'Flaherty VC: A Recruiting Pamphlet* (1915) **(p. 132)**

R. C. Sherriff, *Journey's End* (1928) **(pp. 109, 132)**

Peter Whelan, *The Accrington Pals* (1982) **(p. 134)**

TEXTS IN TRANSLATION
Dates indicate the first publication of the work in the original language.

Henri Barbusse (French), *Under Fire* (1916) **(p. 54)**

Marc Dugain (French), *The Officer's Ward* (1998) **(p. 125)**

Jaroslav Hašek (Czech), *The Good Soldier Švejk* (1923) **(p. 125)**

Ernst Jünger (German), *Storm of Steel* (1920) **(p. 125)**

Erich Maria Remarque (German), *All Quiet on the Western Front* (1929) **(pp. 109, 133)**

LITERARY TERMS

alliteration the repetition of the same consonant or a sequence of vowels in a stretch of language, most often at the beginnings of words or on **stressed** syllables

allusion a passing reference in a work of literature to something outside itself, such as another work of literature, a legend, a cultural belief or a historical fact

ambiguity the capacity of words and sentences to have double, multiple or uncertain meanings

anapaest a kind of **rhythm** in which a three-syllable metrical **foot** is made up of two unstressed syllables followed by a **stressed** syllable (ti-ti-tum), as seen in May Wedderburn Cannan's 'Rouen'

anaphora a **rhetorical** device in which a word or group of words is repeated at the start of a series of sentences, phrases or lines of poetry

assonance the use of the same vowel sound with different consonants or the same consonant with different vowel sounds in successive words or **stressed** syllables in a line of verse

avant-garde writers, painters, musicians, etc., who are considered the most modern or advanced for their time (the term was originally a military one, meaning the vanguard – troops sent on ahead)

ballad a traditional poem or song which tells a story in simple, **colloquial** language, often told through dialogue and action; stylistic features typically include **refrains** and repetition

bathos a descent from a point of high **rhetoric** to the trivial or ridiculous

blank verse unrhymed **iambic pentameter**

caesura a pause about the middle of a line of verse, generally indicated by a pause in the sense

calligram a poem in which the typography and layout is part of the overall effect; the term was coined by Guillaume Apollinaire (also known as a **shape-poem**)

chiasmus a **rhetorical** device where two phrases are related to each other through a reversal in the word order, for example in Yeats's 'An Irish Airman foresees His Death': 'The years to come seemed *waste of breath*, / A *waste of breath* the years behind'

chivalry a code of behaviour followed by medieval knights, including courage, honour, justice and help for the weak (the term is often nowadays confined to mean courtesy and protectiveness especially towards women)

chorus this term has several meanings: the recurring **refrain** in a song (such as that imitated in Sorley's 'All the hills and vales along'), a choir of singers, or a voice, or group of voices, commenting on events

cliché a widely used expression which, through over-use, has lost impact and originality

colloquial the kinds of expression and grammar associated with ordinary, everyday speech rather than formal language

couplet a pair of rhymed lines of any **metre**

elegy a poem of lamentation, usually focusing on the death of a single person

enjambement (or *enjambment*) when a sentence runs on from one line to the next or even from one **stanza** to the next

epic a long narrative poem recounting heroic acts in the history of a people or nation

epitaph originally an inscription on a gravestone it can also be a short commemorative speech or piece of writing about a dead person

euphemism an inoffensive word or phrase substituted for one considered offensive or hurtful

foot a combination of strong **stress** and weak stress or stresses which makes up the **metre** of a line of poetry

free verse unrhymed verse without a standard **metre,** used extensively by **modernist** poets such as Eliot and Pound

half-rhyme another name for **pararhyme**

iambic pentameter a line of poetry consisting of five iambic **feet** (an iambic foot consists of a weakly **stressed** syllable followed by a strongly stressed one)

imagery descriptive language which uses images to make actions, objects and characters more vivid in the reader's mind. **Metaphors** and **similes** are examples of imagery

LITERARY TERMS

Imagism a literary movement in Britain and the USA initiated by Ezra Pound and T. E. Hulme around 1910; Richard Aldington was another member of the group. Imagists valued directness of language in short lyric poems, usually constructed around single **images**, and exploiting juxtaposition

impressionistic based on the personal impressions of an observer or participant rather than an attempt to create a unified account

irony the humorous or sarcastic use of words to imply the opposite of what they normally mean; incongruity between what might be expected and what actually happens; the ill-timed arrival of an event that had been hoped for

martial rhetoric the exalted language of the warrior, used to encourage military action

metaphor a figure of speech in which a word or phrase is applied to an object, a character or an action which does not literally belong to it, in order to imply a resemblance and create an unusual or striking **image** in the reader's mind

metre the pattern of **stresses** occurring (more or less regularly) in lines of poetry and arranged within a fixed total number of syllables. Stressed and unstressed syllables are combined to form a metrical **foot**

modernism a term applied to experimental trends in literature and the other arts in the early and mid-twentieth century; in poetry the reader is often challenged to deduce meaning from a collage of fragmentary **images** and complex **allusions**

monologue originally, a long speech by one actor in a play; applied to poetry it refers to an account in the voice of one person

motif a recurring idea in a work, which is used to draw the reader's attention to a particular theme or topic

narrative a story, tale or any recital of events, and the manner in which it is told

narrator the voice telling the story or relating a sequence of events

octave (or octet) the eight-line opening section of a Petrarchan **sonnet**

onomatopoeia the use of words whose sounds echo the noises they describe

oratorical typical of an orator or public speaker, especially in using **rhetoric**

oxymoron a **rhetorical** figure of speech in which contradictory terms are used together for emphasis

paradox a seemingly absurd or self-contradictory statement that is or may be true

pararhyme half-rhymes, such as Owen's ending of successive lines in 'Exposure' with 'snow-dazed' and 'sun-dozed'

parody an imitation of a work of literature or a literary style designed to ridicule the original

pastoral originally referring to literature that expressed longing for the simplicity of the life of shepherds and other country folk, this can now mean any work which contrasts the simple and the complicated life, though often still with a sense of the beauty of nature

pathos the power of arousing feelings of pity and sorrow in a work

persona an identity assumed by a writer in a literary work; a means of writing from a perspective not one's own

personification the treatment or description of an object or an idea as human, with human attributes and feelings

realism description of things as they are; in literature, a style that avoids representing life in an idealised or heroic manner

refrain words or lines recurring at intervals in the course of a poem, sometimes with slight variation, usually at the end of a **stanza**; they are especially common in songs and **ballads**

register style of language suitable for a particular situation (such as a formal register)

rhetoric the art of persuasive speaking or writing

rhyme chiming or matching sounds, usually at the ends of lines of poetry, which create an audible sense of pattern

rhythm the variation in levels of **stress** accorded to the syllables in a particular stretch of language; in poetry the rhythm is more or less controlled and regular (see **metre**)

romance in addition to its other meanings, **romance** describes a narrative (in prose or verse) from the Middle Ages about the exciting adventures of chivalrous heroes

Romantic when given a capital letter, Romantic refers to a period in English literary history from around 1789 (the French Revolution) to about 1830. Principal English Romantic writers include Wordsworth, Coleridge, Keats and Shelley; the Romantic movement rejected tradition and placed great emphasis on the poet's feelings, on responses to nature and on the power of the imagination

satire a type of literature in which folly, evil or topical issues are held up to scorn through ridicule, irony or exaggeration

sestet the six-line conclusion of a Petrarchan **sonnet**

shape-poem a poem in which the shape reflects in some way the subject matter; see also **calligram**

sibilance words or letters pronounced with a hissing sound

simile a figure of speech which compares two things using the words 'like' or 'as'

sonnet a poem consisting of fourteen lines of **iambic pentameter** which are rhymed and organised according to one of several intricate schemes. The Italian or Petrarchan sonnet consists of an **octave** (eight lines) and a **sestet** (six lines); the Shakespearean sonnet has three quatrains (four lines each) and a final **couplet**

stanza in a poem when lines of verse are grouped together into units these units are called stanzas; they usually follow a pattern with a fixed number of lines and a set number of metrical **feet** within each line

stress in any word of more than one syllable, more emphasis or loudness will be given to one of the syllables in comparison with the others; in English poetry, the **metre** of a line is determined by regular patterns of stressed syllables in a sequence of stressed and unstressed syllables

surrealism a term coined by Apollinaire in 1917 to describe an emphasis on free, creative expression of the artist's or writer's unconscious; typified by free association of ideas, non-logical order and dream-like or nightmarish sequences.

symbolism investing material objects with abstract powers and meanings greater than their own; allowing a complex idea to be represented by a single object

synonym a word that means the same or nearly the same as another word

Tom Rank has a degree in English and a Graduate Certificate in Education from Leeds University, together with a Master's degree in Education from the University of Manchester. After a period in Pakistan with Voluntary Service Overseas, Tom taught in England for many years, becoming a Head of English at secondary level. He is a senior examiner and principal moderator for one of the major A Level English Literature specifications, as well as a freelance writer and consultant. He is the author of the York Notes Advanced title on Sheridan's *The School for Scandal*.

Guillaume Apollinaire, excerpts from 'Calligram', reproduced by kind permission of Oliver Bernard

Herbert Asquith, excerpts from 'The Volunteer', from *Poems 1912–13*, reproduced by permission of Pan Macmillan, London © Herbert Asquith, 1934

Laurence Binyon, excerpts from 'For the Fallen', reproduced by kind permission of the Society of Authors, Literary Representative of the Estate of Laurence Binyon

John Peale Bishop, excerpts from 'In the Dordogne', reproduced by kind permission of Dr Jonathan Bishop

Edmund Blunden, excerpts from 'The Zonnebeke Road' and 'Vlamertinghe: Passing the Château, July 1917' (© Edmund Blunden) are reproduced by permission of PFD (www.pfd.co.uk) on behalf of Edmund Blunden

May Wedderburn Cannan, excerpts from 'Rouen', reproduced by kind permission of Major Cannan Slater

E. E. Cummings, excerpts from 'next to of course god america i', are reprinted from *Complete Poems 1904–1962*, by E. E. Cummings, edited by George J. Firmage, by permission of W. W. Norton & Company. Copyright © 1991 by the Trustees for the E. E. Cummings Trust and George James Firmage

Elizabeth Daryush, excerpts from 'Subalterns', from *The Oxford Book of War Poetry*, 1984, reproduced by permission of Carcanet Press Limited

T. S. Eliot, excerpts from 'Triumphal March', 'Corian I' in *Collected Poems 1909–1962* by T. S. Eliot, copyright 1936 by Houghton Mifflin Harcourt Publishing Company and renewed 1964 by T. S. Eliot, reprinted by permission of Houghton Mifflin, and Faber & Faber Ltd on Behalf of the Estate of T. S. Eliot

Robert Frost, excerpts from 'Range-Finding, from *The Poetry of Robert Frost* edited by Edward Connery Lathem, published by Jonathan Cape. Copyright 1916, 1969 by Henry Holt and Company. Copyright 1944 by Robert Frost. Reprinted by permission of Henry Holt and Company, LLC and The Random House Group Ltd

Robert Graves, excerpts from 'Recalling War' and 'The Persian Version', from *Complete Poems in One Volume*, 2000, reproduced by permission of Carcanet Press Limited

Julian Grenfell, excerpts from 'Into Battle', reproduced by kind permission of Hertfordshire Archives and Local Studies. Document reference: D/Ex 789/F23A

Ivor Gurney, excerpts from 'To His Love', 'The Ballad of Three Spectres' and 'The Silent One', from *Collected Poems*, 2004, reproduced by permission of Carcanet Press Limited

Ted Hughes, excerpts from 'Six Young Men', from *Selected Poems 1957–1994*. Copyright © 2002 by the Estate of Ted Hughes. Reproduced by permission of Farrar, Straus and Giroux LLC, and Faber & Faber, Ltd

David Jones, excerpts from *In Parenthesis*, 1937, reproduced by kind permission of Faber & Faber Ltd and Mr Anthony Hyne

Rudyard Kipling, excerpts from 'Epitaphs of the War', reproduced by permission of A P Watt Ltd on behalf of The National Trust for Places of Historic Interest or Natural Beauty

Philip Larkin, excerpts from 'MCMXIV', from *Collected Poems*. Copyright © 1988, 2003 by the Estate of Philip Larkin. Reproduced by permission of Farrar, Straus and Giroux LLC, and Faber & Faber, Ltd

Wilfred Owen, 'Anthem for Doomed Youth', 'Dulce Et Decorum Est', 'Exposure', 'Insensibility' and 'Strange Meeting' are included in *Wilfred Owen: The Complete Poems and Fragments*, ed. by Jon Stallworthy (London: Chatto & Windus, 1983)

Ezra Pound, excerpts from *Hugh Selwyn Mauberley*, from *Personae*, copyright 1926 © by Ezra Pound, reproduced by kind permission of New Directions Publishing Corp., and Faber & Faber Ltd on behalf of the Estate of Ezra Pound

Edgell Rickword, excerpts from 'Winter Warfare' from *Collected Poems*, 1991, reproduced by permission of Carcanet Press Limited

Carl Sandburg, excerpts from 'Grass' in *Cornhuskers* by Carl Sandburg, copyright 1918 by Holt, Rinehart and Winston and renewed 1946 by Carl Sandburg, reprinted by permission of Houghton Mifflin Harcourt Publishing Company

Siegfried Sassoon, excerpts from 'The Hero', 'The Rear-Guard', copyright 1918 by E. P. Dutton. Copyright renewed 1946 by Siegfried Sassoon. 'The General', 'Glory of Women', from *Collected Poems of Siegfried Sassoon*, copyright 1918, 1920 by E. P. Dutton. Copyright 1936, 1946, 1947, 1948, 1966 by Siegfried Sassoon. Used by kind permission of Viking Penguin, a division of Penguin Group USA (Inc.), and the Estate of George Sassoon

W. B. Yeats, excerpts from 'Easter 1916' and 'An Irish Airman Foresees His Death', reproduced by permission of A P Watt Ltd on behalf of Gráinne Yeats